Glories of Thy Wondrous Name

From Sri Prema-vivarta
of Śrīla Jagadānanda Paṇḍita

Edited By
Dr. Sahadeva dasa
B.com., CA., ICWA., PhD
Chartered Accountant

Soul Science University Press

www.vedictexts.com

Readers interested in the subject matter of this
book are invited to correspond with the publisher at:
SoulScienceUniversity@gmail.com +91 98490 95990
or visit DrDasa.com

First Edition: August 2014

Soul Science University Press expresses its gratitude to the
Bhaktivedanta Book Trust International (BBT), for the use of quotes by
His Divine Grace A.C.Bhaktivedanta Swami Prabhupada.

ISBN 97893-82947-16-5

Published by:
Dr. Sahadeva dasa for Soul Science University Press

Printed by:
Rainbow Print Pack, Hyderabad

To order a copy write to purnabramhadasa@gmail.com
or buy online: Amazon.com, rlbdeshop.com

Dedicated to....

His Divine Grace A.C.Bhaktivedanta Swami Prabhupada

Our saṅkīrtana movement was first introduced in New York in 1966. At that time I came and began to chant this Hare Kṛṣṇa mantra in Tompkins Square. I was chanting there for three hours with a small mṛdaṅga (drum), and these American boys assembled and gradually joined, and so it is increasing.... We are attracting many students simply by chanting, and they are understanding the entire philosophy and becoming purified. This Society's movement started only four years ago, in 1966, and we have so many branches already. The American boys and girls are taking it very seriously, and they are happy. Ask any one of them. Ceto-darpaṇa-mārjanam [Cc. Antya 20.12]. They are cleansing the dirty things from the heart, simply by chanting Hare Kṛṣṇa, Hare Kṛṣṇa, Kṛṣṇa Kṛṣṇa, Hare Hare/ Hare Rāma, Hare Rāma, Rāma Rāma, Hare Hare.

~Srila Prabhupada (Science of Self Realization)

By The Same Author

Oil-Final Countdown To A Global Crisis And Its Solutions

End of Modern Civilization And Alternative Future

To Kill Cow Means To End Human Civilization

Cow And Humanity - Made For Each Other

Cows Are Cool - Love 'Em!

Let's Be Friends - A Curious, Calm Cow

Wondrous Glories of Vraja

We Feel Just Like You Do

Tsunami Of Diseases Headed Our Way - Know Your Food Before Time Runs Out

Cow Killing And Beef Export - The Master Plan To Turn India Into A Desert By 2050

Capitalism Communism And Cowism - A New Economics For The 21st Century

Noble Cow - Munching Grass, Looking Curious And Just Hanging Around

World - Through The Eyes Of Scriptures

To Save Time Is To Lengthen Life

Life Is Nothing But Time - Time Is Life, Life Is Time

Lost Time Is Never Found Again

Spare Us Some Carcasses - An Appeal From The Vultures

An Inch of Time Can Not Be Bought With A Mile of Gold

Cow Dung For Food Security And Survival of Human Race

Cow Dung - A Down-To-Earth Solution To Global Warming And Climate Change

(More information on availability on DrDasa.com)

Preface

Since time immemorial, in every continent and in every major organized and pagan religion, followers have used a string of beads to chant repetitive, uplifting sonic phrases to help create a sense of calm and purpose in life. Most common among these phrases are the ones that refer to names of God and chanting of these names is probably the single most important religious practice that cuts across all religion, culture and civilization lines.

Names of God, known as Holy Names, is a form of addressing God present in liturgy or prayer of various world religions. This has been established as most common spiritual practice in Western and Eastern spiritual practices. A number of traditions have lists of many names of God which enumerate His various qualities. The Qur'an contains the Ninety-nine Names of Allah. Judaism refers to 72 Divine Names and Mahabharata text contains a thousand names of Vishnu.

There are scriptural references for that in all religions because every genuine religious tradition in the world teaches that God's names are holy and meant to be glorified.

When teaching his disciples how to pray, Jesus Christ glorified God's holy name: Our Father, who art in Heaven, hallowed be

Thy name. (Matthew 6:9) Jesus also approved of his disciples' singing joyfully in praise of God. (Luke 19:36-40) Of his own name, Jesus said: For where two or three are gathered together in my name, I am there with them. (Matthew 18:20)

The Bible contains numerous references to glorifying God and His holy name. (Exodus 15:3; Deuteronomy 32:2-3; I Chronicles 16:8-36; Psalms 29:2, 47:1, 86:11, 91:14, 96:1-3, 97:12, 98:4-6, 113:3, 116:1-17, 146:1, 148:1-5, 13)

The Lord and His name are praised throughout the Psalms. I will praise the name of God with a song, says King David. (Psalm 69:30) In other places we read: All nations whom Thou hast made shall come and worship before Thee, O Lord: and shall glorify Thy name. (Psalm 86:9)

In Judaism, the name of God is more than a distinguishing title; it represents the Jewish conception of the divine nature, and of the relationship of God to the Jewish people and to the world. To demonstrate the sacredness of the names of God, and as a means of showing respect and reverence for them, the scribes of sacred texts treat them with absolute sanctity when writing and speaking them. The various titles for God in Judaism represent God as He is known, as well as the divine aspects which are attributed to Him. YHWH is the proper name of God in the Tanakh.

Islam: Praise the Name of the Lord, the Most High who hath created and completely formed His creatures and who determineth them to various ends and driveth them to attain the same.(Al Quran)

Sikhism: Sing and Praise His endless attributes. Singing and listening to His Name and keeping Love for Him in mind will make sorrows disappear and happiness will appear, wherever you be. (Guru Nanak)

God according to Guru Nanak has endless number of virtues; takes on innumerable forms; and can be called by an infinite number of names. Thus Your Names are so many, and Your Forms are endless. No one can tell how many Glorious Virtues You have. (Guru Granth Sahib p. 358)

Vedic Tradition: In this age of quarrel and hypocrisy the only means of deliverance is chanting the holy name of the Lord. There is no other way. There is no other way. There is no other way. (Bṛhan-nāradīya Purāṇa)

Buddhism: If there are good men or good women who hear of Amitabha Buddha, and recite his name single mindedly and without confusion, for one day or two days or three days or four days or five days or six days or seven days, then when these people are about to die, Amitabha Buddha and all the sages who are with him will appear before them. When these people die, their minds will not fall into delusion, and they will attain rebirth in Amitabha Buddha's Land of Ultimate Bliss. (The Amitabha Sutra)

Since the earliest of times, people have used pebbles or a string of nots or beads on a cord to keep track of prayers offered to God.

Known commonly as Mantra Beads, this is an ancient tool that we can use to bring harmony in the opposing energies within body, mind, intellect and innermost spiritual nature.

Sahadeva dasa

Dr Sahadeva dasa
1st August 2014
Secunderabad, India

Introduction

This book is based on a 16th century classic, Prema-vivarta by Srila Jagadananda Pandita. The original work is in Bengali which is mostly spoken in the Eastern part of India. The author was an associate of Sri Chaitanya Mahaprabhu who was a notable proponent of the Vaishnava school of Bhakti yoga (loving devotion to God), based on the philosophy of the Bhagavata Purana and Bhagavad Gita.

Sri Chaitanya Mahaprabhu was a social reformer from 16th century India, revered by his followers as the Supreme Being. He founded the Achintya Bheda Abheda school of Vedanta. Specifically, he worshipped Krishna, popularised the chanting of the Hare Krishna mantra and composed the Siksastakam (eight devotional prayers) in Sanskrit. His followers, Gaudiya Vaishnavas, revere him as an avatar of Krishna in the mood of His consort Radha.

Srila Jagadananda Pandita was a close and confidential associate of Lord Chaitanya. A resident of Navadvipa, he was Lord Chaitanya's boyhood friend and classmate. They enjoyed a unique relationship throughout life. He was continually picking fights with the Lord. These quarrels began from their early boyhood days and continued in Jagannatha Puri. By then Lord Chaitanya had already entered the sannyasa order of life. Their seemingly acrimonious demeanour stemmed from a deep concern for each other and not from self-aggrandizement. Their dealings were enacted on the transcendental plane of pure consciousness.

The book Prema-vivarta delineates the Lord's exemplary Vaisnava dealings and His preaching activities in a simple, lucid Bengali. In fact there are few literatures that can boast of an easy, direct and unequivocal presentation of complex esoteric concepts.

This present work utilizes a widely available translation of this Bengali classic and great care has been taken to carefully edit and correct it.

The editor hopes this book will do its bit in filling the spiritual void in today's fast-paced lives.

Glories of Thy Wondrous Name

একদিন কৃষ্ণদাস কাশীমিশ্রের ঘরে।
আপন গৌহারি কিছু কহিল প্রভুরে।।
আজ্ঞা হয় শুনি কৃষ্ণনামের মহিমা।
যে মহিমার ব্রহ্মা শিব নাহি জানে সীমা।।

nāma mahimā

eka dina kṛṣṇa dāsa kāśī miśrera ghare |
āpana gauhāri kichu kahila prabhure ||*1*||
ājñā haya śuni kṛṣṇa nāmera mahimā |
ye mahimāra brahmā śiva nāhi jāne sīmā ||2||

One day Kṛṣṇadāsa, in Kāśī Miśra's house enquired from Lord Chaitanya, 'Kindly describe the wondrous glories of kṛṣṇa's name. These glories are unlimited and even great demigods like Lord Brahmā and Lord Śiva have not been able to understand their superexcellence completely.'

প্রভু বলে,—"কৃষ্ণনামের মহিমা অপার।
কৃষ্ণ নিজে নাহি জানে, কি জানিব জীব ছার।।
শাস্ত্রে যাহা শুনিয়াছি কহিব তোমারে।
বিশ্বাস করিয়া শুন যাবে ভবপারে।।

prabhu bale kṛṣṇa nāmera mahimā apāra |
kṛṣṇa nije nāhi jāne ki jāniba jīva chāra ||3||

śāstre yāhā śuniyāchi kahiba tomāre |
viśvāsa kariyā śuna yābe bhava pāre ||4||

Lord Caitanya replied, The superexcellence of the holy name is like an ever-expanding ocean. Even Lord Kṛṣṇa Himself does not know the limits of It, what to speak of ordinary living entities. I will simply repeat what I have heard from the scriptures. Any one who hears this with faith, will crossover this ocean of birth and death.

সর্ব্বপাপপ্রশমক সর্ব্বব্যাধিনাশ।
সর্ব্বদুঃখবিনাশন কলিবাধাহ্রাস।।
নারকি-উদ্ধার আর প্রারব্ধখণ্ডন।
সর্ব্বঅপরাধ-ক্ষয় নামে সর্ব্বক্ষণ।।
সর্ব্ব-সৎ-কর্ম্মের পূর্ত্তি নামের বিলাস।
সর্ব্ববেদাধিক নামসূর্য্যের প্রকাশ।।
সর্ব্বতীর্থের অধিক নাম সর্ব্বশাস্ত্রে কয়।
সকল সৎকর্ম্মাধিক্য নামেতে উদয়।।

sarva pāpa praśamaka sarva vyādhi nāśa |
sarva duḥkha vināśana kali bādhā hrāsa ||5||
nāraki uddhāra āra prārabdha khaṇḍana |
sarva aparādha kṣaya nāme sarva kṣaṇa ||6||
sarva sat karmera pūrti nāmera vilāsa |
sarva vedādhika nāma sūryera prakāśa ||7||
sarva tīrthera adhika nāma sarva śāstra kaya |
sakala sat karmādhikya nāmete udaya ||8||

The holy name delivers a living entity from all kinds of sinful reactions and it is a cure for all the maladies, material and spiritual. Chanting is a way out from all pains and miseries of this world and it saves one from the dangerous faults of Kaliyuga.

Krsna's name releases sinners from hellish sufferings and wipes out karma from the previous births. With every recitation, it liberates one from all offenses committed knowingly or unknowingly.

Holy name is the quintessence of all auspicious activities. It is the topmost mantra to be found in the Vedic literatures and it shines like the brillian Sun, destroying the darkness within and without.

Krsna's name is more than the sum total of all holy places and it is the summum bonum of all pious deeds.

সর্ব্বার্থপ্রদাতা নাম, সর্ব্বশক্তিময়।
জগৎ-আনন্দকারী নামের ধর্ম্ম হয়।।
নাম লঞা জগদ্বন্দ্য হয় সর্ব্বজন।
অগতির গতি নাম পতিতপাবন।।

sarvārtha pradātā nāma sarva śakti maya |
jagat ānanda kārī nāmera dharma haya ||9||
nāma lañā jagad-vandya haya sarva jana |
agatira gati nāma patita pāvana ||10||

The holy name is omnipotent and grants the devotee all benedictions. It is like a desire tree that fulfills all desires. When the Sun of Krsna's name rises, the world is filled with transcendental bliss. A person who chants the holy name becomes worshipable by the whole world.

সর্ব্বত্র সর্ব্বদা সেব্য সর্ব্বমুক্তিদাতা।
বৈকুণ্ঠপ্রাপক নাম হরিপ্রীতিদাতা।।
নাম স্বয়ং পুরুষার্থ ভক্ত্যঙ্গপ্রধান।
শ্রুতি-স্মৃতি-শাস্ত্রে আছে বহুত প্রমাণ।।

sarvatra sarvadā sevya sarva mukti dātā |
vaikuṇṭha prāpaka nāma hari prīti dātā ||11||
nāma svayaṁ puruṣārtha bhakty-aṅga-pradhāna |
śruti-smṛti-śāstre āche bahuta pramāṇa ||12||

Holy name is all worshipable and should be served in all places and at all times. It is the giver of liberations of all description, including elevation to the supreme spiritual abode. Transcendental love of Godhead is the ultimate benediction granted by the holy name.

Among all different processes of bhakti, the holy name stands supreme. It is the ultimate destination for all spiritual aspirants and all scriptures glorify its sublime position.

নাম সর্ব্বপাপবিনাশক

সর্ব্বপাপনাশ করা নামের একধর্ম্ম।
প্রথমে তাহাই সপ্রমাণ শুন মর্ম্ম।।
পাপী অজামিল দেখ বিবশ হইয়া।
হরিনাম উচ্চারিল 'নারায়ণ' বলিয়া।।
কোটি কোটি জন্মে পাপ করিয়াছে যত।
সে সকল হইতে মুক্ত হইল সাম্প্রত।।

nāma sarva pāpa vināśaka

sarva pāpa nāśa karā nāmera eka dharma |
prathame tāhā-i sa-pramāṇa śuna marma ||13||
pāpī ajāmila dekha vivaśa haiyā |
harināma uccārila nārāyaṇa baliyā ||14||
koṭi koṭi janme pāpa kariyāche yata |
se sakala haite mukta haila sāmprata ||15||

The Holy Name destroys all sins:

One of the inherent characteristics of the holy name is that It destroys all sins. Hear how Ajamila, a great sinner was delivered. On his deathbed, he unconsciously called out, 'Nārāyaṇa'. Immediately he was freed from innumerable sins he had committed in millions of lifetimes.

অয়ং হি কৃতনির্ব্বেশো জন্মকোট্যংহসামপি।
যদ্ব্যাজহার বিবশো নাম স্বস্ত্যয়নং হরেঃ।। (ভাঃ ৬।২।৭)

ayaṁ hi kṛta-nirveśo janma-koṭy-aṁhasām api |
yad vyājahāra vivaśo nāma svasty-ayanaṁ hareḥ ||16||
[BhP 6.2.7, HBV 11.331]

Ajāmila has already atoned for all his sinful actions. Indeed, he has atoned not only for sins performed in one life but for those performed in millions of lives, for in a helpless condition he chanted the holy name of Nārāyaṇa. Even though he did not chant purely, he chanted without offense, and therefore he is now pure and eligible for liberation. (Srimad Bhagavatam)

স্ত্রী-রাজ-গো-ব্রাহ্মণ-ঘাতী মদ্যরত।
গুরুপত্নীগামী মিত্রদ্রোহী চৌর্য্যব্রত।।
এ সবের পাপ আর অন্য পাপচয়।
হরিনাম উচ্চারণে সব পরিষ্কৃত হয়।।
পাপ সুনিষ্কৃত হৈলে কৃষ্ণে হয় মতি।
এইরূপে নামে জীবের হয় ত সদ্‌গতি।।

strī rāja go brāhmaṇa ghātī madya rata |
guru patnī gāmī mitra drohī caurya vrata ||17||

e sabera pāpa āra anya pāpa caya |
harināma uccāraṇe saba pariṣkṛta haya ||18||
pāpa suniṣkṛta haile kṛṣṇe haya mati |
ei rūpe nāme jīvera haya ta sad-gati ||19||

Even the grievous sins like murdering a woman, a king, a cow or a brāhmaṇa; taking intoxicants, cohabiting with guru's wife, betraying a friend, stealing etc. are easily counteracted by chanting the holy name. When one is freed from sinful reactions, he develops his attachment to Krsna. In this way the holy name liberates a living entity.

স্তেনঃ সুরাপো মিত্রধ্রুগ্ ব্রহ্মহা গুরুতল্পগঃ।
স্ত্রীরাজপিতৃগোহন্তা যে চ পাতকিনোঽপরে।।
সর্ব্বেষামপ্যঘবতামিদমেব সুনিষ্কৃতম্।
নামব্যাহরণং বিষ্ণোর্যতস্তদ্বিষয়া মতিঃ।।(ভা ৬।২।৯-১০)

stenaḥ surā-po mitra-dhrug brahma-hā guru-talpa-gaḥ |
strī-rāja-pitṛ-go-hantā ye ca pātakino 'pare ||20||
sarveṣām apy aghavatām idam eva suniṣkṛtam |
nāma-vyāharaṇaṁ viṣṇor yatas tad-viṣayā matiḥ ||21||
[BhP 6.2.9-10, HBV 11.332-3]

The chanting of the holy names of Lord Viṣṇu is the best process of atonement for a thief of gold or other valuables, for a drunkard, for one who betrays a friend or relative, for one who kills a brāhmaṇa, or for one who indulges in sex with the wife of his guru, or another superior. It is also the best method of atonement for one who murders women, the king or his father, for one who slaughters cows, and for all other sinful men. Simply by chanting the holy name of Lord Viṣṇu, such sinful persons may attract the attention of the Supreme Lord, who therefore considers, 'Because this man has chanted My holy name, My duty is to give him protection.'

ব্রতাদি নামের নিকট তুচ্ছ

চান্দ্রায়ণব্রত-আদি শাস্ত্রোক্ত প্রকারে।
পাপ হইতে পাপীকে নাহি সেরূপ নিস্তারে।।
কৃষ্ণনাম একবার উচ্চারিত যবে।
সর্ব্বপাপ হইতে পাপী মুক্ত হয় তবে।।

vratādi nāmera nikaṭa tuccha

cāndrāyaṇa-vrata ādi śāstrokta prakāre |
pāpa haite pāpīke nāhi se rūpa nistāre ||22||
kṛṣṇa nāma eka bāra uccārita yabe |
sarva pāpa haite pāpī mukta haya tabe ||23||

Penances and vows are insignificant compared to chanting:

Observing penances and vows like candrayana-vrata, strictly according to scriptural injunctions cannot completely eradicate the sins of a sinner. Yet, by chanting Kṛṣṇa's name even once, one becomes totally free from all sins.

ন নিষ্কৃতৈরুদিতৈর্ব্রহ্মবাদিভি-
স্তথা বিশুধ্যত্যঘবান্ ব্রতাদিভিঃ।।
যথা হরের্নামপদৈরুদাহৃতৈ-
স্তদুত্তমঃশ্লোকগুণোপলম্ভকম্।। (ভা ৬।২।১১)

na niṣkṛtair uditair brahma-vādibhis
tathā viśuddhyaty aghavān vratādibhiḥ |
yathā harer nāma-padair udāhṛtais
tad uttamaśloka-guṇopalambhakam ||24||
[BhP 6.12.11, HBV 11.334]

By following the Vedic ritualistic ceremonies or undergoing atonement, sinful men do not become as purified as by chanting once the holy name of Lord Hari. Although ritualistic atonement may free one from sinful reactions, it does not awaken devotional service, unlike the chanting of the Lord's names, which reminds one of the Lord's fame, qualities, attributes, pastimes and paraphernalia.

সঙ্কেতে বা হেলায় নাম গ্রহণ

সঙ্কেত বা পরিহাস স্তোভ হেলা করি'।
নামাভাসে কভু যদি বলে 'কৃষ্ণ' 'হরি'।।
অশেষপাতক তার দূরে যায় তবে।
শ্রীবৈকুণ্ঠে নীত হয় যমদূতের পরাভবে।।

saṅketa vā parihāsa stobha helā kari |
nāmābhāse kabhu yadi bale kṛṣṇa hari ||25||
aśeṣa pātaka tāra dūre yāya tabe |
śrī-vaikuṇṭhe nīta haya yamadūtera parābhave ||26||

Even if a person chants the holy name unconsciously or indirectly, in a joking mood or derision, or even in neglectful disregard, all his innumerable sins are destroys and he becomes fit to enter the spiritual realm of Vaikuntha which lies beyond the jurisdiction of Yamaraja, the god of death.

সাঙ্কেত্যং পারিহাস্যং বা স্তোভং হেলনমেব বা।
বৈকুণ্ঠনামগ্রহণমশেষাঘহরং বিদুঃ।। (ভা ৬।২।১৪)

sāṅketyaṁ pārihāsyaṁ vā stobhaṁ helanam eva vā |
vaikuṇṭha-nāma-grahaṇam aśeṣāgha-haraṁ viduḥ ||27||
[BhP 6.2.14, HBV 11.335]

One who chants the holy name of the Lord is immediately freed from the reactions of unlimited sins, even if he chants indirectly [to indicate something else], jokingly, for musical entertainment, or even neglectfully. This is accepted by all the learned scholars of the scriptures.

পড়ি' খসি' ভগ্ন দষ্ট দগ্ধ বা আহত।
হইয়া বিবশে বলে 'আমি হৈনু হত'।।
'কৃষ্ণ' 'হরি' 'নারায়ণ' নাম মুখে ডাকে।
যাতনা কখন আশ্রয় না করে তাহাকে।।
পতিতঃ স্খলিতো ভগ্নঃ সন্দষ্টস্তপ্ত আহতঃ।
হরিরিত্যবশেনাহ পুমান্নর্হতি যাতনাঃ।। (ভা ৬।২।১৫)

paḍi khasi bhagna daṣṭa dagdha vā āhata |
haiyā vivaśe bale āmi hainu hata ||28||
kṛṣṇa hari nārāyaṇa nāma mukhe ḍāke |
yātanā kakhana āśraya nā kare tāhāke ||29||
patitaḥ skhalito bhagnaḥ sandaṣṭas tapta āhataḥ |
harir ity avaśenāha pumān nārhati yātanāḥ ||30||
[BhP 6.2.15, HBV 11.336]

If one chants the holy name of Hari and then dies because of an accidental misfortune, such as falling from the top of a house, slipping and suffering broken bones while traveling on the road, being bitten by a serpent, being afflicted with pain and high fever, or being injured by a weapon, he is immediately absolved from having to enter hellish life, even though he is sinful.

জ্ঞানে বা অজ্ঞানে নাম

অজ্ঞানে বা জ্ঞানে কৃষ্ণনাম-সংকীর্ত্তনে।
সর্ব্ব পাপ ভস্ম হয়, যথা কাষ্ঠ অগ্ন্যর্পণে।।

অজ্ঞানাদথবা জ্ঞানাদুত্তমঃশ্লোকনাম যৎ।
সংকীর্ত্তিতমঘং পুংসো দহেদেধো যথানলঃ।।
(ভা ৬।২।১৮)

jñāne vā ajñāne nāma

ajñāne vā jñāne kṛṣṇa nāma saṅkīrtane |
sarva pāpa bhasma haya yathā kāṣṭha agny-arpaṇe ||31||
ajñānād athavā jñānād uttamaśloka-nāma yat |
saṅkīrtitam aghaṁ puṁso dahed edho yathānalaḥ ||32||
[BhP 6.2.18, HBV 11.337]

As a fire burns dry grass to ashes, so the holy name of the Lord, whether chanted knowingly or unknowingly, burns to ashes without fail, all the reactions of one's sinful activities.

প্রারব্ধ অপ্রারব্ধ সমস্ত পাপনাশ

বর্ত্তমান পাপ আর পূর্ব্ব-জন্মার্জ্জিত।
ভবিষ্যতে হ'বে যাহা সে সকল হত।।
অনায়াসে হবে কৃষ্ণনাম-সংকীর্ত্তনে।
নাম বিনা বন্ধু নাহি জীবের জীবনে।।
বর্ত্তমানন্তু যৎ পাপং যদ্ভূতং যদ্ভবিষ্যতি।
তৎসর্ব্বং নির্দ্দহত্যাশু গোবিন্দ-কীর্ত্তনানলঃ।।
(লঘু ভাঃ)

prārabdha aprārabdha samasta pāpa nāśa

vartamāna pāpa āra pūrva janmārjita |
bhaviṣyate habe yāhā se sakala hata ||33||
anāyāse habe kṛṣṇa nāma saṅkīrtane |
nāma vinā bandhu nāhi jīvera jīvane ||34||
vartamānaṁ tu yat pāpaṁ yad bhūtaṁ yad bhaviṣyati |

tat sarvaṁ nirdahaty āśu govindānala-kīrtanāt ||35||
[LaghuBhā, HBV 11.339]

Holy name is the only real friend of the living entity. By chanting the holy name, one easily uproots all sinful reactions that have accumulated not only in this lifetime but in many past lives as well and which are yet to mature into fruition.

দ্রোহকারীর মুক্তি

মহীতলে সজ্জনের প্রতি পাপাচারে।
নামকীর্ত্তনেতে মুক্তি লভে সর্ব্ব নরে।।
সদা দ্রোহপরো যস্তু সজ্জনানাং মহীতলে।
জায়তে পবনো ধন্যো হরের্নামানুকীর্ত্তনাৎ।। **(লঘু ভাঃ)**

drohakārīra mukti

mahītale sajjanera prati pāpācāre |
nāma kīrtanete mukti labhe sarva nare ||36||
sadā droha-paro yas tu sajjanānāṁ mahī-tale |
jāyate pāvano dhanyo harer nāmānukīrtanāt ||37||
[LaghuBhā, HBV 11.340]

Those who needlessly offend the innocent and pious citizens, can atone this great sin by chanting the holy name of Kṛṣṇa.

কোটি প্রায়শ্চিত্ত নামতুল্য নহে

শাস্ত্রে কোটি কোটি প্রায়শ্চিত্ত আছে কহে।
কিন্তু কৃষ্ণকীর্ত্তনের তুল্য কেহ নহে।।
বসন্তি যানি কোটিস্তু পাবনানি মহীতলে।
ন তানি তত্তুল্যং যান্তি কৃষ্ণনামানুকীর্ত্তনে।। **(কূর্ম্ম পুঃ)**

koṭi prāyaścitta nāma tulya nahe

śāstre koṭi koṭi prāyaścitta āche kahe |
kintu kṛṣṇa kīrtanera tulya keha nahe ||38||
vasanti yāni koṭis tu pāvanāni mahītale |
na tāni tat-tulāṁ yānti kṛṣṇa-nāmānukīrtane ||39||
[KurmaP, HBV 11.341]

Scriptures recommend countless types of atonements for countless varieties of sins, but all these are inconsequential compared to the chanting of the holy name.

নামগ্রহণকারীর পাপ থাকে না

হরিনাম যত পাপ নির্হরণ করে।
তত পাপ পাপী কভু করিতে না পারে।।
নাম্নোঽস্য যাবতী শক্তিঃ পাপ-নির্হরণে হরেঃ।
তাবৎ কর্ত্তুং ন শক্নোতি পাতকং পাতকী জনঃ।। (কূর্ম্ম পুঃ)

nāma-grahaṇa kārīra pāpa thāke nā

harināma yata pāpa nirharaṇa kare |
tata pāpa pāpī kabhu karite nā pāre ||40||
nāmno'sya yāvatī śaktiḥ pāpa-nirharaṇe hareḥ |
tāvat kartuṁ na śaknoti pātakaṁ pātakī janaḥ ||41||
[kurma-purāṇe HBV 11.342||

Simply by chanting one holy name of Hari, a sinful man can counteract the reactions to more sins than he is able to commit.

মনোবাক্‌কায়জ পাপ তত নাহি হয়।
কলিতে গোবিন্দ-নামে যত হয় ক্ষয়।।

তন্নাস্তি কর্ম্মজং লোক-বাগ্‌জং মানসমেব বা।
যন্ন ক্ষপয়তে পাপং কলৌ গোবিন্দকীর্ত্তনম্।। (স্কন্দ পুঃ)

mano-vāk-kāya-ja pāpa tata nāhi haya |
kalite govinda nāme nāhi haya kṣaya ||42||
tan nāsti karmajaṁ loke vāg-jaṁ mānasam eva vā |
yan na kṣapayate pāpaṁ kalau govinda-kīrtanam ||43||
[skānda, HBV 11.344]

In this age of Kali, all varities of sins, committed by body, mind or words, can be counteracted simply by chanting the name of Govinda.

নামে সর্ব্বরোগ নাশ হয়

নামে সর্ব্বব্যাধিধ্বংস সর্ব্বশাস্ত্রে গায়।
ওগো স্থানেশ্বরী ভক্ত বলিহে তোমায়।।
সত্য সত্য বলি, লহ বিশ্বাস করিয়া।
'অচ্যুতানন্দ' 'গোবিন্দ' এই নাম উচ্চারিয়া।।
কাঁদিয়া কাঁদিয়া ডাক শ্রীমধুসূদনে।
সর্ব্বরোগ নাশ করে শ্রীনামকীর্ত্তনে।।
অচ্যুতানন্দ-গোবিন্দ-নামোচ্চারণভাষিতাঃ।
নশ্যন্তি সকলা রোগাঃ সত্যং সত্যং বদাম্যহম্।। (বৃহন্নারদীয়)

nāme sarva-roga nāśa haya

nāme sarva vyādhi dhvaṁsa sarva śāstre gāya |
ogo sthānesvarī bhakta bali he tomāya ||44||
satya satya bali laha viśvāsa kariyā |
acyutānanda govinda ei nāma uccāriyā ||45||
kāṅdiyā kāṅdiyā ḍāka śrī madhusūdana |
acyutānanda-govinda-nāmoccaraṇa-bhīṣitaḥ |

naśyanti sakalā rogāḥ satyaṁ satyaṁ vadāmy aham ||46||
[bṛhan-nāradīya HBV 11.353||

Scriptures proclaim that the holy name is the only cure for all material diseases and sufferings. O residents of Puri, I emphatically declare unto you to have full faith and chant the names of Krsna, feelingly from the heart with tears of love flowing from your eyes.

নামে মহাপতকীও পংক্তিপাবন হয়

মহাপাতকীও অহর্নিশ হরিগানে।
শুদ্ধ হঞা গণ্য হয় সুপংক্তিপাবনে।।
মহাপাতকযুক্তোঽপি কীর্ত্তয়ন্ননীশং হরিম্।
শুদ্ধান্তঃকরণো ভূত্বা জায়তে পংক্তিপাবনঃ।। (ব্রহ্মাণ্ড পু)

nāme mahā pātakī paṅkti pāvana haya

mahā pātakī-o aharniśa hari gāne |
śuddha hañā gaṇya haya supaṅkti pāvane ||47||
mahā-pātaka-yukto'pi kīrtayenn aniśaṁ harim |
śuddhāntaḥkaraṇo bhūtvā jāyate paṅkti-pāvanaḥ ||48||
[brahmāṇḍa, HBV 11.348]

When even the most deleterious person engages in continuous chanting of harināma, the deepest core of his heart is cleansed, and soon he ranks amongst the best of the twice-born brāhmaṇas, able to purify others.

ভয় ও দণ্ড-নিবারণ

মহাব্যাধি-ভয়ও বা রাজদণ্ড-ভয়।
নারায়ণ-সঙ্কীর্ত্তনে নিরাতঙ্ক হয়।।

মহাব্যাধি-সমাচ্ছন্নো রাজবাধোপপীড়িতঃ।
নারায়ণেতি সঙ্কীর্ত্ত্য নিরাতঙ্কো ভবেন্নরঃ। (বহ্নি পু)

bhaya o daṇḍa nivāraṇa

mahā vyādhi bhaya o vā rāja daṇḍa bhaya |
nārāyaṇa saṅkīrtane nirātaṅka haya ||49||
mahā-vyādhi-samācchanno rāja-vadhopāpiditaḥ |
nārāyaṇeti saṅkīrtya nirāṭaṅko bhaven naraḥ ||50||
[vahni-purāṇe HBV 11.356]

All dreadful sufferings and sicknesses are easily quelled by chanting of Lord Nārāyaṇa's name.

সর্ব্বরোগ-সর্ব্বক্লেশ-উপদ্রব-সনে।
অরিষ্টাদি-বিনাশ হয় হরি-উচ্চারণে।।
সর্ব্বরোগোপশমনং সর্ব্বোপদ্রবনাশনম্।
শান্তিদং সর্ব্বারিষ্টানাং হরের্নামানুকীর্ত্তনম্।। (বৃহদ্ বি পু)

sarva-roga sarva-kleśa upadrava sane |
ariṣṭādi-vināśa haya hari uccāraṇe ||51||
sarva-rogopaśamanaṁ sarvopadrava-nāśanam |
śāntidaṁ sarvāriṣṭānāṁ harer nāmānukīrtanam ||52||
[[bṛhad-viṣṇu-purāṇe HBV 11.357||

Constant chanting of harināma is extremely beneficial and auspicious because it destroys all diseases, distresses and impediments.

যথা অতিবায়ুবলে মেঘ দূরে যায়।
সূর্য্যোদয়ে তমোনাশ অবশ্যই পায়।।
তথা সঙ্কীর্ত্তিত নাম জীবের ব্যসন।
দূর করে স্বপ্রভাবে, এ ব্যাসবচন।।
সংকীর্ত্ত্যমানো ভগবাননন্তঃ।
শ্রুতানুভাবো ব্যসনং হি পুংসাম্।
প্রবিশ্য চিত্তং বিধুনোত্যশেষং
যথা তমোঽর্কোঽভ্রমিবাতিবাতঃ।। (ভা ১২।১২।৪৮)

yathā ati vāyu bale megha dūre yāya |
sūryodaye tamo nāśa avaśya-i pāya ||53||
tathā saṅkīrtita nāma jīvera vyasana |
dūra kare sva-prabhāve e vyāsa-vacana ||54||
saṅkīrtyamāno bhagavān anantaḥ
śrutanubhāvo vyasanaṁ hi puṁsām |
praviśya cittaṁ vidhunoty aśeṣaṁ
yathā tamo'rko'bhram ivāti-vātaḥ ||55||
[BhP 12.12.48, HBV 11.359]

When people properly chant the name of the Supreme Lord or simply hear about His power, the Lord personally enters their hearts and cleanses away every trace of misfortune, just as the sun removes the darkness or as a powerful wind drives away the clouds.

This is explained by Śrīla Vyasadeva in the Śrīmad-Bhāgavatam.

আর্ত্ত বা বিষণ্ন শিথিলমনা ভীত।
ঘোরব্যাধিক্লেশে আর না দেখে হিত।।

'নারায়ণ' 'হরি' বলি' করে সঙ্কীর্ত্তন।
নিশ্চয় বিমুক্তদুঃখ সুখী সেই জন।।
আর্ত্তা বিষণ্ণাঃ শিথিলাশ্চ ভীতা
ঘোরেষু চ ব্যাধিষু বর্ত্তমানাঃ।
সংকীর্ত্ত্য নারায়ণ-শব্দমেকং
বিমুক্তদুঃখা সুখিনো ভবন্তি।। (বিষ্ণুধর্ম্মোত্তর)

ārta vā viṣaṇṇa śithila-manā bhīta |
ghora-vyādhi-kleśe āra nā dekhe hita ||56||
nārāyaṇa hari bali kare saṅkīrtana |
niścaya vimukta-duḥkha sukhī sei jana ||57||
ārtā viṣaṇṇāḥ śithilāś ca bhītā
ghoreṣu ca vyādhiṣu vartamānāḥ |
saṅkīrtya nārāyaṇa-śabdam ekaṁ
vimukta-duḥkhāḥ sukhino bhavanti ||58||

People who are deeply tormented by poverty, hopelessness, despondency, weakness of mind, fear and serious diseases rarely see a ray of hope but if they simply chant the name of Hari, they will be released from their intolerable misery and experience unlimited happiness.

[viṣṇu-dharmottare HBV 11.360]

অসীম শক্তিমান্ বিষ্ণু, তাঁহার কীর্ত্তনে
যক্ষ-রক্ষ-বেতালাদি ভূতপ্রেতগণে।।
বিনায়ক-ডাকিন্যাদি হিংস্রক সমস্ত।
পলায়ন করে সব দুঃখ হয় অস্ত।।
সর্ব্বানর্থনাশী হরিনাম সঙ্কীর্ত্তন।
ক্ষুধা তৃষ্ণা স্খলিতাদি বিপদনাশন।।

asīma śaktimān viṣṇu tāṅhāra kīrtane |

yakṣa rakṣa vetālādi bhūta preta gaṇe ||59||
vināyaka ḍakinyādi hiṁsraka samasta |
palāyana kare saba duḥkha haya asta ||60||
sarvānartha-nāśī harināma saṅkīrtana |
kṣudhā tṛṣṇā skhalitādi vipada-nāśana ||61||

The holy name of Viṣṇu possesses unlimited power and inconceivable potencies. When the holy name is uttered, all evil spirits, ghosts, witches, demons and monsters flee in fear. Chanting removes all inauspiciousness, tribulations, hunger, thirst, confusions and so on.

ইহাতে সংশয় যথা, নিশ্চয় তথায়।
নামের বিক্রম কভু না হয় উদয়।।
বিশ্বাসে নামের কৃপা, অবিশ্বাসে নয়।
এ এক রহস্য, ভক্ত জানহ নিশ্চয়।।

ihāte saṁśaya yathā niścaya tathāya |
nāmera vikrama kabhu nā haya udaya ||62||
viśvāse nāmera kṛpā aviśvāse naya |
e eka rahasya bhakta jānaha niścaya ||63||

In spite of knowing all these facts about the name's potency, if one still doubts Its efficacy, he will not achieve any success in chanting. One receives the mercy of the holy name only by increasing one's faith and not by faithless doubting.

কীর্ত্তনাদ্দেবদেবস্য বিষ্ণোরমিততেজসঃ।
যক্ষরাক্ষসবেতালভূতপ্রেতবিনায়কাঃ।।
ডাকিন্যো বিদ্রবন্তি স্ম যে তথান্যে চ হিংসকাঃ।
সর্ব্বানর্থহরং তস্য নামসংকীর্ত্তনং স্মৃতম্।।

নামসংকীর্ত্তনং কৃত্বা ক্ষুত্তৃট্ প্রস্খলিতাদিষু।
বিয়োগং শীঘ্রমাপ্নোতি সর্ব্বানর্থৈর্ন সংশয়ঃ।। (বিষ্ণুধর্ম্মোত্তর)

kīrtanad deva-devasya viṣṇor amita-tejasaḥ |
yakṣa-rakṣasa-vetala-bhūta-preta-vinayakaḥ ||64||
dakinyo vidravanti sma ye tathānye ca siṁhakaḥ |
sarvānartha-haraṁ tasya nāma-saṅkīrtanaṁ smṛtam ||65||
nāma-saṅkīrtanaṁ kṛtvā kṣuṭ-tṛṭ-praskhalitādiṣu |
viyogam śīghram āpnoti sarvānarthair na saṁśayaḥ ||66||
[viṣṇu-dharmottare HBV 11.361-3]

These verses have been explained in the previous five verses.

কলিকালকুসর্পের তীক্ষ্ণ দংষ্ট্রা হেরি'।
ভয় না করিও ভক্ত, শুন শ্রদ্ধা করি'।।
কৃষ্ণনাম-দাবানল প্রজ্জ্বলিত হঞা।
সে সর্পের দংষ্ট্রা দগ্ধ করিবে ফেলিয়া।।
কলিকালকুসর্পস্য তীক্ষ্ণদংষ্ট্রস্য মা ভয়ম্।
গোবিন্দনামদাবেন দগ্ধো যাস্যতি ভস্মতাম্।। (স্কন্দ পু)

kali kāla kusarpera tīkṣna daṁṣṭrā heri |
bhaya nā kario bhakta śuna śraddhā kari ||67||
kṛṣṇa nāma dāvānala prajjvalita hañā |
se sarpera daṁṣṭrā dagdha karibe pheliyā ||68||
kali-kala-ku-sarpasya tīkṣṇa-daṁṣṭrasya mā bhayam |
govinda-nāma-dāvena dagdho yāsyati bhasmatām ||69||
[skānda, HBV 11.365]

Dear devotees! I see that Kali-yuga is like a black, poisonous serpent with a gaping mouth and sharp fangs. But please be unperturbed. The forest fire of kṛṣṇa's name immediately burns to ashes this poisonous snake and its ferocious fangs.

এই ঘোর কলিযুগে হরিনামাশ্রয়ে।
কৃতকৃত্য ভক্তগণ ত্যক্ত-অন্যাশ্রয়ে।।
হরে কেশব গোবিন্দ বাসুদেব জগন্ময়।
এই নাম সঙ্কীর্ত্তনে বড় সুখোদয়।।
সদা যেই গায় নাম বিশ্বাস করিয়া।
কলিবাধা নাহি তা'র সদা শুদ্ধ হিয়া।।
হরিনামপরা যে চ ঘোরে কলিযুগে নরাঃ।
তে এব কৃতকৃত্যাশ্চ ন কলির্বাধতে হি তান্।।
হরে কেশব গোবিন্দ বাসুদেব জগন্ময়।
ইতীরয়ন্তি যে নিত্যং ন হি তান্ বাধতে কলিঃ।। (বৃহন্নারদীয়ে)

ei ghora kali-yuge hari nāmāśraye |
kṛta kṛtya bhakta gaṇa tyakta anyāśraye ||70||
hare keśava govinda vāsudeva jaganmaya |
ei nāma saṅkīrtane baḍa sukhodaya ||71||
sadā yei gāya nāma viśvāsa kariyā |
kali bādhā nāhi tāra sadā śuddha hiyā ||72||
hari-nāma-parā ye ca ghore kali-yuge narāḥ |
ta eva kṛta-kṛtyāś ca na kalir bādhate hi tān ||73||
hare keśava govinda vāsudeva jagan-maya |
itīrayanti te nityaṁ na hi tān bādhate kaliḥ ||74||
[bṛhannāradīya, HBV 11.366-7]

In this dark age of Kali, learned and sincere devotees of the Lord should leave aside all other means of self realization and take full shelter of the holy name. This is their prime duty. There is great transcendental bliss in the names of Kṛṣṇa. For one who chants constantly with unflinching faith, his heart always remains pure and contamination of kaliyuga never touches him.

নারকী কীর্ত্তন করে 'হরি' 'কৃষ্ণ' বলি'।
হরিভক্ত হঞা যায় দিব্যধামে চলি'।।
যথা তথা হরের্নাম কীর্ত্তয়ন্তি স্ম নারকাঃ।
তথা তথা হরৌ ভক্তিমুদ্বহন্তো দিব্যং যযুঃ।। (নারসিংহ)

nārakī kīrtana kare hari kṛṣṇa bali |
hari bhakta hañā yāya divya dhāme cali ||75||
yathā yathā harer nāma kīrtayanti sma nārakāḥ |
tathā tathā harau bhaktim udvahanto divaṁ yayuḥ ||76||
[nārasiṁhe HBV 11.369]

An abominable sinner, a candidate for hellish life can easily become a devotee of the Lord simply by chanting Kṛṣṇa's name. Thus he can enter into the transcendental abode of the Lord.

প্রারব্ধখণ্ডন কেবল হরিনামে হয়।
জ্ঞানকর্ম্মে সেই ফল কভু না মিলয়।।
বিনা হরিকীর্ত্তন কভু কর্ম্মবন্ধ।
খণ্ডন না হয়, মুমুক্ষুতা নহে লব্ধ।।
যে মুক্তি লভিলে আর না হয় কর্ম্মসঙ্গ।
রজঃস্তমোদোষহীন শূন্য মায়াসঙ্গ।।
নাতঃ পরং কর্ম্মনিবন্ধকৃন্তনং
মুমুক্ষতাং তীর্থপদানুকীর্ত্তনাৎ।
ন যৎ পুনঃ কর্ম্মসু সজ্জতে মনো-
রজস্তমোভ্যাং কলিলং ততোঽন্যথা।। (ভা ৬।২।৪৬)

prārabdha-khaṇḍana kevala hari nāme haya |
jñāna-karme sei phala kabhu nā milaya ||77||
vinā hari kīrtana kabhu karma bandha |
khaṇḍana nā haya mumukṣutā nahe labdha ||78||
ye mukti labhile āra nā haya karma saṅga |
rajas tamo doṣa hīna śūnya māyā-saṅga ||79||
nātaḥ paraṁ karma-nibandha-kṛntanaṁ
mumukṣatāṁ tīrtha-padānukīrtanāt |
na yat punaḥ karmasu sajjate mano
rajas-tamobhyāṁ kalilaṁ tato'nyathā ||80||
[BhP 6.2.46, HBV 11.371]

Therefore one who desires freedom from material bondage should adopt the process of chanting and glorifying the name, fame, form and pastimes of the Supreme Personality of Godhead, at whose feet all the holy places reside. One cannot derive the proper benefit from other methods, such as pious atonement, speculative knowledge and meditation in mystic yoga, because even after following such methods one takes to fruitive activities again, unable to control his mind which is contaminated by the lower qualities of nature, namely passion and ignorance.

ম্রিয়মাণ ক্লিষ্ট জন পড়িতে খসিতে।
বিবশ হইয়া কৃষ্ণ বলে কোনমতে।।
কর্ম্মার্গলমুক্ত হঞা লভে পরা গতি।
কলিকালে যাহা নাহি লভে অন্য মতি।।
যন্নামধেয়ং ম্রিয়মাণ আতুরঃ
পতন্ স্খলন্ বা বিবশো গৃণন্ পুমান্।
বিমুক্তকর্ম্মার্গল উত্তমাং গতিং
প্রাপ্নোতি যক্ষ্যন্তি ন তং কলৌ জনাঃ।। (ভা ১২।৩।৪৪)

mriyamāṇa kliṣṭa jana paḍite khasite |
vivaśa haiyā kṛṣṇa bale kona mate ||81||
karmārgala mukta hañā labhe parā gati |
kali kāle yāhā nāhi labhe anya mati ||82||
yan-nāma-dheyaṁ mriyamāṇa āturaḥ
patan skhalan vā vivaśo gṛṇan pumān |
vimukta-karmārgala uttamāṁ gatiṁ
prāpnoti yakṣyanti na taṁ kalau janāḥ ||83||
[BhP 12.3.44, HBV 11.372]

Terrified, about to die, a man collapses on his bed. Although his voice is faltering and he is hardly conscious of what he is saying, if he utters the holy name of the Supreme Lord he can be freed from the reaction of his fruitive work and achieve the supreme destination. But still the people in this age of Kali will not worship the Supreme Lord.

শ্রদ্ধা করি' নাম লইলে অপরাধকোটী।
ক্ষমা করে কৃষ্ণ, যদি না থাকে কুটিনাটী।।
ইহাতে বিশ্বাস যার না হয়, সে জন।
বড়ই দুর্ভাগা, তা'র নাহিক মোচন।।
মম নামানি লোকেঽস্মিন্ শ্রদ্ধয়া যস্তু কীর্ত্তয়েৎ।
তস্যাপরাধকোটীস্তু ক্ষমাম্যেবং ন সংশয়ঃ।। (বিষ্ণুযামল)

śraddhā kari nāma laile aparādha koṭī |
kṣamā kare kṛṣṇa yadi nā thāke kuṭināṭī ||84||
ihāte viśvāsa yāra nā haya se jana |
baḍa-i durbhāgā tāra nāhika mocana ||85||
mama nāmāni loke'smin śraddhayā yas tu kīrtayet |
tasyāparādha-koṭis tu kṣamāmy eva na saṁśayaḥ ||86||
[viṣṇu-yāmale HBV 11.375]

If a person chants the holy name with faith and devotion and his heart is free from diplomacy and duplicity, kṛṣṇa forgives his countless offenses. An unfortunate soul who has no faith in the holy name can never be delivered by any means.

মন্ত্র-তন্ত্র-ছিদ্র দেশ-কাল-বস্তু-দোষ।
নামসঙ্কীর্ত্তনে যায়, পায় পরম সন্তোষ।।
সৎকর্ম্মপ্রধান নাম, তাহার আশ্রয়ে।
অন্য সৎকর্ম্মের সিদ্ধি হইবে নিশ্চয়ে।।
মন্ত্রতস্তন্ত্রতশ্ছিদ্রং দেশকালার্হবস্তুতঃ।
সর্ব্বং করোতি নিশ্ছিদ্রং নামসঙ্কীর্ত্তনং তব।। (ভা ৮।২৩।১৬)

mantra tantra chidra deśa kāla vastu doṣa |
nāma saṅkīrtane yāya pāya parama santoṣa ||87||
sat karma pradhāna nāma tāhāra āśraye |
anya sat karmera siddhi haibe niścaye ||88||
mantratas tantrataś chidraṁ deśa-kālārha-vastutaḥ |
sarvaṁ karoti niśchidram anusaṅkīrtanaṁ tava ||89||
[BhP 8.23.16, HBV 11.376]

There may be discrepancies in pronouncing the mantras and observing the regulative principles, and, moreover, there may be discrepancies in regard to time, place, person and paraphernalia. But when kṛṣṇa's holy name is chanted, everything becomes faultless.

Chanting is the most important of all spiritual activities, so if one takes shelter of the holy name he will automatically achieve perfection in all other devotional endeavours.

সর্ব্ববেদাধিক নাম, ইহাতে সংশয়।
যে করে তাহার কভু মঙ্গল না হয়।।

প্রণব কৃষ্ণের নাম যাহা হৈতে বেদ।
জন্মিল ব্রহ্মার মুখে বুঝ তত্ত্বভেদ।।
ঋক্-যজু-সামাথর্ব্ব সে কৈল পঠন।
'হরি' 'হরি' যার মুখে শুনি' অনুক্ষণ।।
ঋগ্বেদো হি যজুর্ব্বেদঃ সামবেদোপ্যথর্ব্বণঃ।
অধীতাস্তেন যেনোক্তং হরিরিত্যক্ষরদ্বয়ম্।। (বিষ্ণুধর্ম্মোত্তর)

sarva vedādhika nāma ihāte saṁśaya |
ye kare tāhāra kabhu maṅgala nā haya ||90||
praṇava kṛṣṇera nāma yāhā haite veda |
janmila brahmāra mukhe bujha tattva bheda ||91||
ṛk-yaju-sāmātharva se kaila paṭhana |
hari hari yāra mukhe śuni anukṣaṇa ||92||
rg-vedo hi yajur-vedaḥ sāma-vedo'py atharvaṇaḥ |
adhītas tena yenoktaṁ harir ity akṣara-dvayam ||93||
[viṣṇu-dharmottare, HBV 11.378]

The holy name of kṛṣṇa is superior to all the Vedic mantras. Anyone who doubts this conclusion never achieves any auspiciousness.

Pranava or Omkar (Om) is one of Kṛṣṇa's names; Vedic mantras have emanated from this seed, manifesting first from the lotus mouth of Brahmā, the self-born. One who always utters the two syllables Hari is considered to have studied all the four Vedas.

ঋক্-যজু-সামাথর্ব্ব পঠ কি কারণ।
'গোবিন্দ' 'গোবিন্দ' নাম করহ কীর্ত্তন।।
মা ঋচো মা যজুস্তাত মা সাম পঠ কিঞ্চন।
গোবিন্দেতি হরের্নাম গেয়ং গায়স্ব নিত্যশঃ।। (স্কন্দ পুরাণ)

ṛk yaju sāmātharva paṭha ki kāraṇa |
govinda govinda nāma karaha kīrtana ||94||
mā ṛco mā yajus tāta mā sāma paṭha kiṁcana |
govindeti harer nāma geyaṁ gāyasva nityaśaḥ ||95||
[skānde, HBV 11.379 | |

What prompts you to undertake the tedious study of the four Vedas, namely, Rg, Sama, Yajur and Atharva? Simply go on chanting Govinda, Govinda! That's all that is required to achieve perfection.

বিষ্ণুর প্রত্যেক নাম সর্ব্ববেদাধিক।
'রাম'-নাম জান সহস্র নামের অধিক।।
বিষ্ণোরেকৈকনামাপি সর্ব্ববেদাধিকং মতম্।
তাদৃক্ নামসহস্রেণ 'রাম'-নামসমং স্মৃতম্।। (পদ্মপুরাণ)

viṣṇura pratyeka nāma sarva vedādhika |
rāma nāma jāna sahasra nāmera adhika ||96||
viṣṇor ekaika-nāmāpi sarva-vedādhikaṁ matam |
tadṛṅ-nāma-sahasreṇa rāma-nāma samaṁ smṛtam ||97||
[pādme HBV 11.380]

Each name of Lord Viṣṇu is superior and more potent than all the Vedic mantras combined. And one name of Lord Rāma equals thousand such names of Viṣṇu.

সহস্র নাম তিনবার আবৃত্তি করিলে।
যেই ফল হয় তাহা এক কৃষ্ণ-নামে মিলে।।
"কৃষ্ণ কৃষ্ণ কৃষ্ণ কৃষ্ণ কৃষ্ণ কৃষ্ণ কৃষ্ণ হে।"
এই নাম সর্ব্বক্ষণ ভক্ত সব কর হে।।

'হরে কৃষ্ণ হরে কৃষ্ণ কৃষ্ণ কৃষ্ণ হরে হরে।
হরে রাম হরে রাম রাম রাম হরে হরে।।"
এই ষোল নামে সর্ব্বদিক্ বজায় রহিল হে।
সর্ব্বফলসিদ্ধি লাভ এই ষোল নামে হইবে হে।।
সহস্রনাম্নাং পুণ্যানাং ত্রিরাবৃত্ত্যা তু যৎ ফলম্।
একাবৃত্ত্যা তু কৃষ্ণস্য নামৈকং তৎ প্রযচ্ছতি॥ (ব্রহ্মাণ্ড পুরাণ)

sahasra nāma tina bāra āvṛtti karile |
yei phala haya tāhā eka kṛṣṇa nāme mile ||98||
kṛṣṇa kṛṣṇa kṛṣṇa kṛṣṇa kṛṣṇa kṛṣṇa kṛṣṇa he |
ei nāma sarva kṣaṇa bhakta saba kara he ||99||
hare kṛṣṇa hare kṛṣṇa kṛṣṇa kṛṣṇa hare hare |
hare rāma hare rāma rāma rāma hare hare ||100||
ei ṣola nāme sarva dik bajāya rahila he |
sarva phala siddhi lābha ei ṣola nāme haibe he ||101||
sahasra-nāmnāṁ puṇyānāṁ trir-āvṛttyā tu yat phalam |
ekāvṛttyā tu kṛṣṇasya nāmaikaṁ tat prayacchati ||102||
[brahmāṇḍa HBV 11.488]

The spiritual benefit one obtains from chanting a thousand names of Viṣṇu three times is attained by chanting Lord Kṛṣṇa's name just once.

Dear devotees, please chant incessantly, 'Kṛṣṇa, Kṛṣṇa, Kṛṣṇa, Kṛṣṇa, Kṛṣṇa, Kṛṣṇa, he!' And chant, 'Hare Kṛṣṇa, Hare Kṛṣṇa, Kṛṣṇa Kṛṣṇa, Hare Hare; Hare Rama, Hare Rama, Rama Rama, Hare Hare'. This mantra consisting of sixteen names is perfect in every respect, and chanting this mantra awards one the highest benefit and perfection in spiritual life.

তীর্থযাত্রাপরিশ্রমে কিবা ফল হ'বে।
'হরে কৃষ্ণ' নিত্য গানে সব ফল পাবে।।

কিবা কুরুক্ষেত্র, কাশী, পুষ্কর-ভ্রমণে।
জিহ্বাগ্রেতে হরিনাম যাঁ'র ক্ষণে ক্ষণে।।

tīrtha yātrā pariśrame kibā phala habe |
hare kṛṣṇa nitya gāne saba phala pābe ||103||
kibā kurukṣetra kāśī puṣkara bhramaṇe |
jihvāgrete hari nāma yāṅra kṣaṇe kṣaṇe ||104||

Why take the trouble of visiting so many holy places when simply by regular chanting of hare kṛṣṇa mahamantra you can get the benefit of visitng all the holy places in the universe.

কুরুক্ষেত্রেণ কিং তস্য কিং কাশ্যা পুষ্করেণ বা।
জিহ্বাগ্রে বসতি যস্য হরিরিত্যক্ষরদ্বয়ম্।। (স্কন্দ পুরাণ)

kurukṣetreṇa kiṁ tasya kiṁ kāsyā puskareṇa vā |
jihvāgre vasate yasya harir ity akṣara-dvayam ||105||
[skānde HBV 11.381]

There is no use of visiting holy places like Kurukṣetra, Kāśī, Puṣkara for one whose tongue is always decorated with the two syllables of Hari.

কোটি শত কোটি সহস্র তীর্থে যাহা নয়।
হরিনাম-কীর্ত্তনেতে সেই ফল হয়।।
তীর্থকোটিসহস্রাণি তীর্থকোটিশতানি চ।
তানি সর্ব্বাণ্যবাপ্নোতি বিষ্ণোর্নামানুকীর্ত্তনাৎ।। (বামন পু)

koṭi śata koṭi sahasra tīrthe yāhā naya |
harināma kīrtanete sei phala haya ||106||

tīrtha-koṭi-sahasrāṇi tīrtha-koṭi-śatāni ca |
tani sarvāṇy avāpnoti viṣṇor nāmānukīrtanāt ||107||
[vāmana HBV 11.382]

The benefit accrued from chanting of the holy name can not be had by visiting millions or even billions of holy places in the universe.

কুরুক্ষেত্রে বসি' বিশ্বামিত্র ঋষি বলে।
শুনিয়াছি বহু তীর্থনাম ধরাতলে।।
হরিনাম-কীর্ত্তনের কোটি অংশতুল্য।
কোন তীর্থ নাহি—এই বাক্য বহুমূল্য।।
বিশ্রুতানি বহূন্যেব তীর্থানি বিবিধানি চ।
কোট্যংশেন ন তুল্যানি নামকীর্ত্তনতো হরেঃ।। (বিশ্বামিত্র সং)

kurukṣetre basi viśvāmitra ṛṣi bale |
śuniyāchi bahu tīrtha nāma dharātale ||108||
harināma kīrtanera koṭi aṁśa tulya |
kona tīrtha nāhi ei vākya bahu mūlya ||109||
viśrutāṇi bahūny eva tīrthāni bahudhāni ca |
koty-aṁśenāpi tulyāni nāma-kīrtanato hareḥ ||110||
[viśvāmitra-saṁhitā, HBV 11.383]

Once on a visit to Kurukṣetra, the powerful sage Visvamitra said, "I have heard the names of many holy places of pilgrimage in the material universe but rest assured none of them possess even one millionth of the spiritual potency contained in the chanting of the holy name."

বেদাগম বহু শাস্ত্রে কিবা প্রয়োজন।
কেন করে লোক বহুতীর্থাদি ভ্রমণ।।

আত্মমুক্তিবাঞ্ছা যার, সেই সর্ব্বক্ষণ।
'গোবিন্দ' 'গোবিন্দ' বলি' করুক কীর্ত্তন।
কিন্তাত বেদাগমশাস্ত্রবিস্তরৈ-
স্তীর্থৈরনেকৈরপি কিং প্রয়োজনম্।
যদ্যাত্মনো বাঞ্ছসি মুক্তিকারণং
গোবিন্দ গোবিন্দ ইতি স্ফুটং রট।। (লঘু ভাঃ)

vedāgama bahu śāstre kibā prayojana |
kena kare loka bahu tīrthādi bhramaṇa ||111||
ātma-mukti-vāñchā yāra sei sarva-kṣaṇa |
govinda govinda bali karuka kīrtana ||112||
kiṁ tāta vedāgama-śāstra-vistarais
tīrthair anekair api kiṁ prayojanam |
yady ātmano vāñchasi mukti-kāraṇaṁ
govinda govinda iti sphutam raṭa ||113||
[laghu-bhāgavate HBV 11.384]

What is the use of studying such voluminous books like Vedas and their corollaries? And why do people visit innumerable holy places? Anyone desiring deliverance from this material world simply has to sing Govind Govinda always.

সর্ব্বসৎকর্ম্মাধিক নাম জানহ নিশ্চয়।
এই কথা বিশ্বাসিলে সর্ব্বধর্ম্ম হয়।।
সূর্য্য উপরাগে কোটি কোটি গরুদান।
প্রয়াগেতে কল্পবাস মাঘেতে বিধান।।
অযুত যজ্ঞাদি কর্ম্ম স্বর্ণমেরুদান।
শতাংশেতে হরিনামের না হয় সমান।।
গোকোটিদানং গ্রহণে খগস্য প্রয়াগগঙ্গোদক কল্পবাসঃ।
যজ্ঞাযুতং মেরুসুবর্ণদানং গোবিন্দকীর্ত্তের্ন সমং শতাংশৈঃ।।
(লঘু ভাঃ)

sarva-sat-karmādhika nāma jānaha niścaya |
ei kathā viśvāsile sarva dharma haya ||114||
sūrya uparāga koṭi koṭi garu dāna |
prayāgete kalpa vāsa māghete vidhāna ||115||
ayuta yajñādi karma svarga-meru dāna |
śatāṁśete hari nāmera nā haya samāna ||116||
go-koṭi-dānaṁ grahaṇe khagasya
prayāga-gaṅgodaka-kalpa-vāsaḥ |
yajñāyutaṁ meru-suvarṇa-dānaṁ
govinda-kīrter na samaṁ śatāṁśaiḥ ||117||
[laghu-bhāgavate HBV 11.385]

There is no comparison between the holy name and a pious activity. Holy name is vastly superior to all the pious activities in the world. This conclusion is the essence of all religious principles. One who chants with this realization automatically executes all other prescribed religious duties.

Pious activities like giving millions of cows in charity during solar eclipse; residing in Prayaga during the month of Magha (December-January) and observing strict vows; performing countless sacrifices and distributing mountains of gold can not compare to one-ten-thousandth fraction of the holy name's potency.

ইষ্টাপূর্ত্ত কর্ম্ম বহু বহু কৃত হৈলে।
তথাপি সে সব ভবহেতু শাস্ত্রে বলে।।
হরিনাম অনায়াসে ভবমুক্তিধর।
কর্ম্মফল নামের কাছে অকিঞ্চিৎকর।।
ইষ্টাপূর্ত্তানি কর্ম্মাণি সুবহূনি কৃতান্যপি।
ভবহেতূনি তান্যেব হরের্নামতু মুক্তিদম্।। (বোধায়ন সং)

iṣṭa-pūrta karma bahu bahu kṛta haile |
tathāpi se saba bhava hetu śāstre bale ||118||
harināma anāyāse bhava mūkti dhara |
karma phala nāmera kāche akiñcitkara ||119||
iṣṭa-pūrtāni karmāṇi su-bahūni kṛtāny api |
bhava-hetūni tāny eva harer nāma tu muktidam ||120||
[bodhayana-saṁhitā, HBV 11.386]

Even if hundreds of altruistic works are performed for the benefit of the people in general, all such activities will improve the material conditions in this world but the holy name is meant to improve the spiritual condition, i.e., liberation from this material world. These materialistic pious activities are meaningless when compared to the holy name.

সাংখ্যা-অষ্টাঙ্গাদি যোগে কিবা আশা ধর।
মুক্তি চাও—গোবিন্দ-কীর্ত্তন সদা কর।।
মুক্তিও সামান্য ফল নামের নিকটে।
হেলায় করিলে নাম জীবের মুক্তি ঘটে।।
কিং করিষ্যতি সাংখ্যেন কিং যোগৈর্নরনায়ক।
মুক্তিমিচ্ছসি রাজেন্দ্র কুরু গোবিন্দকীর্ত্তনম্।। (গরুড় পু)

sāṅkhya aṣṭāṅgādi yoge kibā āśā dhara |
mukti cāo govinda kīrtana sadā kara ||121||
mukti-o sāmānya phala nāmera nikaṭe |
helāya karile nāma jīvera mukti ghaṭe ||122||
kiṁ kariṣyati sāṅkhyena kiṁ yogair nara-nāyaka |
muktim icchasi rājendra kuru govinda-kīrtanam ||123||
[gāruḍe HBV 11.388]

Why waste your valuable time with saṅkhya-yoga (philosophical speculation) or astanga-yoga (eightfold mystic yoga)! If you desire liberation, simply chant the name of Govinda! Liberation is just an ordinary by-product of the chanting. The holy name easily grants liberation even to some one who chants negligently or in disregard.

শ্বপচ হইলেও দ্বিজশ্রেষ্ঠ বলি তারে।
যাহার জিহ্বাগ্রে কৃষ্ণনাম নৃত্য করে।।
সর্ব্বতপ কৈল সর্ব্বতীর্থে কৈল স্নান।
সর্ব্ববেদ অধ্যয়নে আর্য্য মতিমান্।।
এই সব সাধনের বলে ভাগ্যবান্।
রসনায় সদা করে হরিনাম গান।।
অহো বত শ্বপচোঽতো গরীয়ান্
যজ্জিহ্বাগ্রে বর্ত্ততে নাম তুভ্যম্।
তেপুস্তপস্তে জুহুবুঃ সস্নুরার্য্যা
ব্রহ্মানুচুর্নাম গৃণন্তি যে তে।। (ভাঃ ৩।৩৩।৭)

śvapaca haile-o dvija-śreṣṭha bali tāre |
yāhāra jihvāgre kṛṣṇa-nāma nṛtya kare ||124||
sarva-tapa kaila sarva tīrthe kaila snāna |
sarva veda adhyayane ārya matimān ||125||
ei saba sādhanera bale bhāgyavān |
rasanāya sadā kare harināma gāna ||126||
aho bata śvapaco'to garīyān
yaj-jihvāgre vartate nāma tubhyam |
tepus tapas te juhuvur sasnur aryā
brahmānūcur nāma gṛhṇanti ye te ||127||
[BhP 3.33.7, HBV 11.389]

Oh, how glorious are they whose tongues are chanting Your holy name! Even if born in the families of dog-eaters, such persons are worshipable. Persons who chant the holy name of Your Lordship must have executed all kinds of austerities and fire sacrifices and achieved all the good manners of the Āryans. To be chanting the holy name of Your Lordship, they must have bathed at holy places of pilgrimage, studied the Vedas and fulfilled everything required.

সর্ব্ব-অর্থ-দাতা হরিনাম মহামন্ত্র।
ফুকারিয়া বলে যত বেদাগমতন্ত্র।।
হরিনামবলে সর্ব্বষড়্বর্গ-দমন।
রিপুনিগ্রহণ আর অধ্যাত্ম-সাধন।।
এতৎ ষড়্বর্গহরণং রিপুনিগ্রহণং পরম্।
অধ্যাত্মমূলমেতদ্ধি বিষ্ণোর্নামানুকীর্ত্তনম্।। (স্কন্দ পু)

sarva artha dātā harināma mahāmantra |
phukāriyā bale yata vedāgama tantra ||128||
harināma bale sarva ṣaḍ-varga damana |
ripu nigrahaṇa āra adhyātma sādhana ||129||
etat sad-varga-haraṇam ripu-nigrahaṇaṁ param |
adhyātma-mūlam etad dhi viṣṇor nāmānukīrtanam ||130||
skānde HBV 11.390]

The Hare Kṛṣṇa mahā-mantra is the great chant for deliverance. It fulfills all the aspirations of a living entity and brings him to the highest platform spiritual realization. This fact has been boldly proclaimed in the Vedic literature.

The holy name crushes the six deadly vices - lust, anger, greed, pride, illusion and envy. It pacifies the impetuous senses and enables one to execute devotional service in perfect peace.

গুণজ্ঞ সারভুক্ আর্য্য কলিকে সম্মানে।
সর্ব্বস্বার্থ লভি’ কলৌ নামসঙ্কীর্ত্তনে।।

কলিং সভাজয়ন্ত্যার্য্যা গুণজ্ঞা সারভাগিনঃ।
যত্র সঙ্কীর্ত্তনেনৈব সর্ব্বঃ স্বার্থোঽভিলভ্যতে।। (ভা ১১।৫।৩৬)

guṇajña sāra bhuk ārya kalike sammāne |
sarva svārtha labhi kalau nāma saṅkīrtane ||131||
kaliṁ sabhājayanty āryā guṇa-jāḥ sāra-bhāginaḥ |
yatra saṅkīrtanenaiva sarvaḥ svartho'bhilabhyate ||132||
[BhP 11.5.36, HBV 11.396]

Those who are actually advanced in knowledge are able to appreciate the essential value of this age of Kali. Such enlightened persons worship Kali-yuga because in this fallen age all perfection of life can easily be achieved by the performance of saṅkīrtana.

সর্ব্বশক্তিমান্ নাম কৃষ্ণের সমান।
কৃষ্ণের সকল শক্তি নামে বর্ত্তমান্।।
দানব্রতস্তপস্তীর্থে ছিল যত শক্তি।
দেবগণে কর্ম্মকাণ্ডে হইয়া বিভক্তি।।
রাজসূয়ে অশ্বমেধে আধ্যাত্মিক জ্ঞানে।
সব আকর্ষিয়া কৃষ্ণ নিল আপন নামে।।
দানব্রততপস্তীর্থক্ষেত্রাদীনাঞ্চ যাঃ স্থিতাঃ।
শক্তয়ো দেবমহতাং সর্ব্বপাপহরাঃ শুভাঃ।।
রাজসূয়াশ্বমেধানাং জ্ঞানমধ্যাত্মবস্তুনঃ।
আকৃষ্য হরিণা সর্ব্বাঃ স্থাপিতাঃ স্বেষু নামসু।। (স্কন্দ পু)

sarva śaktimān nāma kṛṣṇera samāna |
kṛṣṇera sakala śakti nāmer vartamāna ||133||
dāna vratas tapas tīrthe chila yata śakti |
deva gaṇe karma kāṇḍe haiyā vibhakti ||134||

rājasūye aśvamedhe ādhyātmika jñāne |
saba ākarṣiyā kṛṣṇa nila āpana nāme ||135||
dāna-vrata-tapas-tīrtha-yātrādīnāṁ ca yāḥ sthitāḥ |
śaktayo deva-mahatāṁ sarva-pāpa-harāḥ śubhāḥ ||136||
rāja-sūyāśvamedhānāṁ jñānasyādhyātma-vastunaḥ |
ākṛṣya hariṇā sarvāḥ sthāpitāḥ sveṣu nāmasu ||137||
[skānde, HBV 11.398-399]

The holy name, like Kṛṣṇa is omnipotent and non-different from him. In these transcendental names, Kṛṣṇa has invested all his transcendental energies.

Whatever spiritual potency was there in auspicious activities like charity, austerity, penances, visiting holy places, karma-kanda rituals offered to the demigods, fire sacrifices like rajasuya and asvamedha, knowledge of self-realization etc, Kṛṣṇa collected these potencies from each of these pious activities and invested in His transcendental name.

দেবদেব শ্রীকৃষ্ণের সর্ব্ব অর্থ শক্তি।
যুক্ত সব নাম, তঁহি মধ্যে যাতে অনুরক্তি।।
সেই নাম সর্ব্ব অর্থে যোজনা করিবে।
সর্ব্ব অর্থ শক্তি হৈতে সকলই মিলিবে।।
সর্ব্বার্থশক্তিযুক্তস্য দেবদেবস্য চক্রিণঃ।
যচ্চাভিরুচিতং নাম তৎ সর্ব্বার্থেষু যোজয়েৎ।। (ব্রহ্মাণ্ড পু)

devadeva śrī-kṛṣṇera sarva artha śakti |
yukta saba nāma taṅhi madhye yāte anurakti ||138||
sei nāma sarva arthe yojanā karibe |
sarva artha śakti haite sakale-i milibe ||139||
sarvārtha-śakti-yuktasya devadevasya cakriṇaḥ |
yac cābhirucitaṁ nāma tat sarvārtheṣu yojayet ||140||
brahmāṇḍe HBV 11.401]

Kṛṣṇa, the master of the demigods has many names and each name is omnipotent and fully capable of fulfilling the goal of life. A devotee may have an attraction to some particular name, so he should gradually increase his attachment to that name and fulfill the mission of his life.

হৃষীকেশ-সঙ্কীর্ত্তনে জগদানন্দিত।
অনুরাগে হৃষ্টচিত্ত সর্ব্বদা সম্প্রীত।।
দৈত্য রক্ষ ভীত হইয়া পলাইয়া যায়।
সিদ্ধসংঘ সদা প্রণমিত তাঁর পায়।।
যেই কৃষ্ণ সেই নাম, নামের প্রভাব।
উপযুক্ত বটে তাতে না থাকে অভাব।।
স্থানে হৃষীকেশ তব প্রকীর্ত্ত্যা।
জগৎ প্রহৃষ্যত্যনুরজ্যতে চ।।
রক্ষাংসি ভীতানি দিশো দ্রবন্তি।
সর্ব্বে নমস্যন্তি চ সিদ্ধসংঘাঃ।। (গীতা ১১।৩৬)

hṛṣīkeśa saṅkīrtane jagad ānandita |
anurāge hṛṣṭa-citta sarvadā samprīta ||141||
daitya rakṣa bhīta haiyā palāiyā yāya |
siddha saṅgha sadā praṇamita tāṅra pāya ||142||
yei kṛṣṇa sei nāma nāmera prabhāva |
upayukta baṭe tāte nā thāke abhāva ||143||
sthāne hṛṣīkeśa tava prakīrtyā
jagat prahṛṣyaty anurajyate ca |
rakṣāṁsi bhītāni diśo dravanti
sarve namasyanti ca siddhasaṁghāḥ ||144||
[gītā 11.36, HBV 11.402]

O master of the senses, the world becomes joyful upon hearing Your name, and thus everyone becomes attached to You. Although the perfected beings offer You their respectful homage, the demons are afraid, and they flee here and there. All this is rightly done.

বর্ণাদি বিচার নাহি শ্রীনামকীর্ত্তনে।
দীক্ষাপুরশ্চর্য্যা বিধি বাধা নাই গণে।।
নারায়ণ জগন্নাথ বাসুদেব জনার্দ্দন।
যার মুখে সদা শুনি, পূজ্য গুরু সেই জন।।
শয়নে স্বপনে আর চলিতে বসিতে।
কৃষ্ণনাম করে যেই, পূজ্য সর্ব্ব মতে।।
নারায়ণ জগন্নাথ বাসুদেব জনার্দ্দন।
ইতীরয়ন্তি যে নিত্যং তে বৈ সর্ব্বত্র বন্দিতাঃ।।
স্বপন্ ভুঞ্জন ব্রজংস্তিষ্ঠনুত্তিষ্ঠংশ্চ বদংস্তথা।
যে বদন্তি হরের্নাম তেভ্যো নিত্যং নামোনমঃ।। (বৃহন্নারদীয়)

varṇādi vicāra nāhi nāma saṅkīrtane |
dīkṣā-puraścaryā vidhi bādhya nāi gaṇe ||145||
nārāyaṇa jagannātha vāsudeva janārdana |
yāra mukhe sadā śuni pūjya guru yei jana ||146||
śayane svapane āra calite basite |
kṛṣṇa-nāma kare yei pūjya sarva mate ||147||
nārāyaṇa jagannātha vāsudeva janārdana |
itīrayanti ye nityaṁ te vai sarvatra vanditāḥ ||148||
svapan bhuñjan vrajaṁs tiṣṭhaṁś ca vadaṁs tathā |
ye vadanti harer nāma tebhyo nityaṁ namo namaḥ ||149||
bṛhan-nāradīye, HBV 11.403-4]

Anyone can chant the holy name, irrespective of his caste or creed. He does not even need formal initiation or vows of purification to be eligible to chant the holy name. Whoever constantly chants the names of the Supreme Lord like Nārāyaṇa, Jagannātha, Vasudeva, Janardana, should be respected by all as a spiritual master. That person who chants Lord Kṛṣṇa's name while sleeping, dreaming, walking or sitting is fit to be worshipped by everyone.

স্ত্রী-শূদ্র-পুক্কশ-যবনাদি কেন নয়।
কৃষ্ণনাম গায়, সেও গুরু পূজ্য হয়।।
স্ত্রী শূদ্রঃ পুক্কশো বাপি যে চান্যে পাপযোনয়ঃ।
কীর্ত্তয়ন্তি হরিং ভক্ত্যা তেভ্যোঽপীহ নামোনমঃ।।
(নারায়ণ-ব্যূহস্তব)

strī-śūdra-pukkaśa-yavanādi kena naya |
kṛṣṇa-nāma gāya seo guru pūjya haya ||150||
strī śūdraḥ pukkaśo vāpi ye cānye pāpa-yonayaḥ |
kīrtayanti hariṁ bhaktyā tebhyo'pīha namo namaḥ ||151||
nārāyaṇa-vyūha-stave, HBV 11.405]

Anyone who chants Lord Kṛṣṇa's name is fit to be worshipped like a guru even though such person may be a woman, a lower class sudra, a pukkasa, a meat-eater or of even lower birth.

(Nārāyaṇa-vyuha-stava)

অন্যগতিশূন্য ভোগী পর-উপতাপী।
ব্রহ্মচর্য্য-জ্ঞানবৈরাগ্যহীন পাপী।।
সর্ব্বধর্ম্মশূন্য নামজপী যদি হয়।
তাহার যে সুগতি তাহা সর্ব্ব ধার্ম্মিকের নয়।।
অনন্যগতয়ো মর্ত্ত্যা ভোগিনোঽপি পরন্তপাঃ।
জ্ঞানবৈরাগ্যরহিতা ব্রহ্মচর্য্যাদিবর্জ্জিতাঃ।।
সর্ব্বধর্ম্মোজ্ঝিতা বিষ্ণোর্নামমাত্রৈকজল্পকাঃ।
সুখেন যাং গতিং যান্তি ন তাং সর্ব্বেঽপি ধার্ম্মিকাঃ।। (পদ্মপু)

anya gati śūnya bhogī para upatāpī |
brahmacarya jñāna vairāgya hīna pāpī ||152||
sarva dharma śūnya nāma japī yadi haya |

tāhāra ye sugati tāhā sarva dhārmikera naya ||153||
ananya-gatayo martyā bhogino'pi parantapāḥ |
jñāna-vairāgya-rahitā brahmacaryādi-varjitāḥ ||154||
sarva-dharmojjhitā viṣṇor nāma-mātraika-jalpakāḥ |
sukhena yāṁ gatiṁ yānti na tāṁ sarve'pi dhārmikāḥ ||155||
pādme, HBV 11.406-7]

One who has no shelter and has no higher goal in life, who is cruel, violent, licentious and bereft of any knowledge, austerity or religious principles, even if he chants the holy name``, he achieves a transcendental destination which the so-called religiously pious people can not even imagine.

হরিনামগ্রহণে দেশকালের নিয়ম নাই।
উচ্ছিষ্ট অশৌচে বিধি নিষেধ না পাই।।
ন দেশনিয়মস্তস্মিন্ ন কালনিয়মস্তথা।
নোচ্ছিষ্টাদৌ নিষেধোঽস্তি শ্রীহরের্নাম্নি লুব্ধক।। (বিষ্ণুধর্ম্ম)

hari nāma grahaṇe deśa kālera niyama nāi |
ucchiṣṭa aśauce vidhi niṣedha nā pāi ||156||
na deśa-niyamas tasmin na kāla-niyamas tathā |
nocchiṣṭhādau niṣedho'sti śrī-harer nāmni lubdhaka ||157||
viṣṇu-dharma, HBV 11.408]

There are no rules indicating time, place or circumstances for chanting the holy name, nor is anyone prohibited from chanting even though he may be unclean or contaminated.

কৃষ্ণনাম সদা সর্ব্বত্র করহ কীর্ত্তন।
অশৌচাদি নাহি মান, নাম স্বতন্ত্র পাবন।।
চক্রায়ুধস্য নামানি সদা সর্ব্বত্র কীর্ত্তয়েৎ।
নাশৌচং কীর্ত্তনে তস্য স পবিত্রকরো যতঃ। (স্কন্দ পু)

kṛṣṇa-nāma sadā sarvatra karaha kīrtana |
aśaucādi nāhi māna nāma svatantra pāvana ||158||
cakrāyudhasya nāmāni sadā sarvatra kīrtayet |
nāśaucaṁ kīrtane tasya sa pavitra-karo yataḥ ||159||
[skānde HBV 11.409||

Just go on chanting Kṛṣṇa's holy name, in all places and at all times. The holy name is completely independent of all material, external rules such as those governing cleanliness. Holy name is a supremely purifying agent—cleansing everything within and without.

যজ্ঞে দানে স্নানে জপে আছে কালের নিয়ম।
কৃষ্ণকীর্ত্তনে কালাকালচিন্তা মহাভ্রম।।
দেশ-কাল-নিয়মাদি নামে কভু নাই।
কৃষ্ণকীর্ত্তন সদা করহ সবাই।।
ন দেশনিয়মো রাজন্ ন কালনিয়মস্তথা।
বিদ্যতে নাত্র সন্দেহো বিষ্ণোর্নামানুকীর্ত্তনে।।
কালোঽস্তি দানে যজ্ঞে চ স্থানে কালোঽস্তি সজ্জপে।
বিষ্ণুসঙ্কীর্ত্তনে কালো নাস্ত্যত্র পৃথিবীতলে।। (বৈষ্ণবচিন্তামণিঃ)

yajñe dāne snāne jape āche kālera niyama |
kṛṣṇa kīrtane kālākāla cintā mahābhrama ||160||
deśa kāla niyamādi nāme kabhu nāi |
kṛṣṇa kīrtana sadā karaha sabāi ||161||
na deśa-niyamo rājan na kāla-niyamas tathā |
vidyate nātra sandeho viṣṇor nāmānukīrtane ||162||
kālo'sti dāne yajñe ca sthāne kālo'sti saj-jape |
viṣṇu-saṅkīrtane kālo nāsty atra pṛthivī-tale ||163||
[vaiṣṇava-cintāmaṇau, HBV 11.412-3]

Pious religious activities like fire sacrifices, charity, sacred baths and chanting of Vedic hymns are regulated by strict rules of time, place and cleanliness. But there are no hard and fast rules for chanting. Anyone, anywhere in any condition or at any time of the day or night, can chant Kṛṣṇa's name. Therefore go on chanting Kṛṣṇa's name without cessation.

সংসারে নির্ব্বিণ্ণচিত্ত অভয়পদ চায়।
হেন যোগীর জন্য নাম একমাত্র উপায়।।
এতান্নির্ব্বিদ্যমানানামিচ্ছতামকুতোভয়ম্।
যোগিনাং নৃপ নির্ণীতং হরের্নামানুকীর্ত্তনম্।। (ভা ২।১।১১)

saṁsāre nirviṇṇa-citte abhya-pada cāya |
hena yogīra janya nāma ekamātra upāya ||164||
etan nirvidyamānānām icchatām akuto-bhayam |
yogināṁ nṛpa nirṇītaṁ harer nāmānukīrtanam ||165||
[BhP 2.1.11, HBV 11.414]

O King, constant chanting of the holy name of the Lord after the ways of the great authorities is the doubtless and fearless way of success for all, including those who are free from all material desires, those who are desirous of all material enjoyment, and also those who are self-satisfied by dint of transcendental knowledge.

হরিনাম বিনা আর সহজ মুক্তিদাতা।
কেহ নাহি ত্রিজগতে, নামই জীবের ত্রাতা।।
একবার মুখে বলে 'হরি' দু'অক্ষর।
সেই জন মোক্ষপ্রতি বদ্ধপরিকর।।
সকৃদুচ্চারিতং যেন হরিরিত্যক্ষরদ্বয়ম্।
বদ্ধঃ পরিকরস্তেন মোক্ষায় গমনং প্রতি।। (স্কন্দ পু)

harināma vinā āra sahaja mukti dātā |
keha nāhi tri jagate nāma-i jīvera trātā ||166||
eka bāra mukhe bale hari du akṣara |
sei jana mokṣa prati baddha parikara ||167||
sakṛd uccāritaṁ yena harir ity akṣara-dvayam |
baddhaḥ parikaras tena mokṣāya gamanaṁ prati ||168||
[skanda-purāṇe, HBV 11.417]

Lord's holy name is the most magnanimous deliverer of conditioned souls. There is no one else who can so easily liberate the fallen souls.

"By once chanting the holy name of the Lord, which consists of the two syllables ha-ri, one guarantees his path to liberation." (Skanda Purāṇa)

জিতনিদ্র হঞা একবার 'নারায়ণ' বলে।
শুদ্ধ-চিত্ত হঞা সেই নির্ব্বাণপথে চলে।।
সুকৃদুচ্চারয়েদ্‌যস্তু নারায়ণমতন্দ্রিতঃ।
শুদ্ধান্তঃকরণো ভূত্বা নির্ব্বাণমধিগচ্ছতি।। (পদ্ম পু)

jita nidra hañā eka bāra nārāyaṇa bale |
śuddha citta hañā sei nirvāṇa pathe cale ||169||
sakṛd uccārayed yas tu nārāyaṇam atandritaḥ |
śuddhāntaḥkaraṇo bhūtvā nirvāṇam adhigacchati ||170||
[brahma-purāṇe, HBV 11.418||

Anyone who chants Lord Nārāyaṇa's name even once with great care and attention, his heart gets cleansed and he proceeds on the path of liberation.

এ ঘোর সংসারে, বলে বিবশে 'হরে হরে'।
সদ্যোমুক্ত হয়, ভয় তারে ভয় করে।।
আপন্নঃ সংসৃতিং ঘোরাং যন্নাম বিবশো গৃণন্।
ততঃ সদ্যো বিমুচ্যেত যদ্বিভেতি স্বয়ং ভয়ম্।। (ভা ১।১।১৪)

e ghora saṁsāre bale vivaśe hare hare |
sadyo mukta haya bhaya tāre bhaya kare ||171||
āpannaḥ saṁsṛtiṁ ghorāṁ yannāma vivaśo gṛṇan |
tataḥ sadyo vimucyeta yad bibheti svayaṁ bhayam ||172||
[BhP 1.1.14, HBV 11.425||

Being tossed about in this dangerous ocean of birth and death, one who chants 'hare hare' even unwillingly, he becomes immediately liberated and fear personified fears him.

"Living beings who are entangled in the complicated meshes of birth and death can be freed immediately by even unconsciously chanting the holy name of Kṛṣṇa, which is feared by fear personified." (Srimad Bhagavatam 1.1.14)

মৃত্যুকালে বিবশে যে করে উচ্চারণ।
তাঁর অবতার নাম লীলা বিড়ম্বন।।
বহুজন্মদুরিত সহসা ত্যাগ করি'।
যায় সে পরমপদে ভজে সেই হরি।।
যস্যাবতারগুণকর্ম্মবিড়ম্বনানি
নামানি যেঽসুবিগমে বিবশা গৃণন্তি।
তেঽনেকজন্মশমলং সহসৈব হিত্বা
সংযান্ত্যপাবৃতমৃতং তমজং প্রপদ্যে।। (ভা ৩।৯।১৫)

mṛtyu-kāle vivaśe ye kare uccāraṇa |
tāṅra avatāra nāma līlā viḍambana ||173||
bahu janma durita sahasā tyāga kari |

yāya se parama pade bhaje sei hari ||174||
yasyāvatāra-guṇa-karma-viḍambanāni
nāmāni ye'su-vigame vivaśā gṛṇanti |
te'naika-janma-śamalaṁ sahasaiva hitvā
saṁyānty apāvṛtāmṛtaṁ tam ajaṁ prapadye ||175||
[BhP 3.9.15, HBV 11.426]

Let me take shelter of the lotus feet of Him whose incarnations, qualities and activities are mysterious imitations of worldly affairs. One who invokes His transcendental names, even unconsciously, at the time of quitting his body, is certainly washed of the sins of many, many births and attains Him without fail.

চলিতে বসিতে স্বপ্নে ভোজনে শয়নে।
কলিদমন কৃষ্ণোচ্চারে বাক্যের পূরণে।।
হেলাতেও করি' নাম নিজ স্বরূপ পাঞা।
পরমপদ বৈকুণ্ঠে যায় নির্ভয় হইয়া।।
ব্রজংস্তিষ্ঠন্ স্বপন্নশ্নন্ শ্বসন্ বাক্যপ্রপূরণে।
নামসঙ্কীর্ত্তনং বিষ্ণোর্হেলয়া কলিবর্ধনম্।
কৃত্বা স্বরূপতাং যাতি ভক্তিযুক্তং পরং ব্রজেৎ।। (লিঙ্গ পু)

calite basite svapne bhojane śayane |
kali damana kṛṣṇoccāre vākyera pūraṇe ||176||
helāte-o kari nāma nija svarūpa pāñā |
parama pada vaikuṇṭhe yāya nirbhaya haiyā ||177||
vrajaṁs tiṣṭhan svapann aśnan śvasan vākya-prapūraṇe |
nāma-saṅkīrtanaṁ viṣṇor helayā kali-mardanam |
kṛtvā svarūpatāṁ yāti bhakti-yuktaṁ paraṁ vrajet ||178||
[laiṅge, HBV 11.428]

In our daily activities of walking, sitting, eating, sleeping and dreaming, chanting Kṛṣṇa's names nullifies the ill effects of Kali-yuga. Even though such chanting may be done neglectfully, it is perfectly capable of liberating us from all fears and elevating us to the supreme abode of Vaikuntha.

যেন তেন প্রকারেতে লয় কৃষ্ণনাম।
তা'কে প্রীতি করে কৃষ্ণ করুণা-নিদান।।
মদ্যপানে ভূতাবিষ্ট বায়ু-পীড়া-স্থলে।
হরিনামোচ্চারে মুক্তি তাঁ'র করতলে।।
বাসুদেবস্য সঙ্কীর্ত্ত্যা সুরাপো ব্যাধিতোঽপি বা।
মুক্তো জায়েত নিয়তং মহাবিষ্ণুঃ প্রসীদতি। (বরাহ পু)

yena tena prakārete laya kṛṣṇa nāma |
tāke prīti kare kṛṣṇa karuṇā nidāna ||179||
madya pāne bhūtāviṣṭa vāyu pīḍā sthale |
hari nāmoccāre mukti tāṅra kara tale ||180||
vāsudevasya saṅkīrtyā surāpo vyādhito'pi vā |
mukto jāyeta niyataṁ mahā-viṣṇuḥ prasīdati ||181||
[vārāhe, HBV 11.442]

If somehow or other one chants Kṛṣṇa's name, Kṛṣṇa is attracted to him and He showers him with His causeless mercy. Even a ghostly haunted drunkard, suffering from numerous health disorders chants the holy name, then liberation is immediately within his reach.

হরিনাম স্বতঃ পরমপুরুষার্থ হয়।
উপেয়-মাঙ্গল্য-তত্ত্ব পরংধনময়।।
জীবনের ফল বস্তু কাশীখণ্ডে বলে।
পদ্মপুরাণেও তাহা কহে বহুস্থলে।।

ইদমেব হি মঙ্গল্যং এতদেব ধনার্জ্জনম্।
জীবিতস্য ফলঞ্চৈতদ্ যদ্দামোদরকীর্ত্তনম্।। (পদ্ম পু)

harināma svataḥ parama puruṣārtha haya |
upeya māṅgalya tattva paraṁ dhana maya ||182||
jīvanera phala vastu kāśī-khaṇḍa bale |
padma-purāṇe-o tāhā kahe bahu sthale ||183||
idam eva hi maṅgalyaṁ etad eva dhanārjanam |
jīvitasya phalaṁ caitad yad dāmodara-kīrtanam ||184||
[padme, HBV 11.450]

Kīrtana of the name of Śrī Dāmodara evokes real auspiciousness and it is the only eternal treasure and only success and aim of human life

সর্ব্ব মঙ্গলের হয় পরম মঙ্গল।
চিত্তত্ত্ব-স্বরূপ সর্ব্ববেদবল্লীফল।।
কৃষ্ণনাম লয় যেই শ্রদ্ধা বা হেলায়।
নর মাত্র ত্রাণ পায় সর্ব্ববেদে গায়।।
মধুরমধুরমেতন্মঙ্গলং মঙ্গলানাং
সকলনিগমবল্লীসৎফলং চিৎস্বরূপম্।
সকৃদপি পরিগীতং শ্রদ্ধয়া হেলয়া বা
ভৃগুবর নরমাত্রং তারয়েৎ কৃষ্ণনাম।। (প্রভাস খণ্ড)

sarva maṅgalera haya parama maṅgala |
cit-tattva svarūpa sarva veda vallī phala ||185||
kṛṣṇa nāma laya yei śraddhā vā helāya |
nara mātra trāṇa pāya sarva vede gāya ||186||
madhura-madhuram etan maṅgalaṁ maṅgalānāṁ
sakala-nigama-vallī-sat-phalaṁ cit-svarūpam |
sakṛd api parigītaṁ śraddhayā helayā vā

bhṛgu-vara nara-mātraṁ tārayet kṛṣṇa-nāma ||187||
[prabhāsa-khaṇḍe, HBV 11.451]

The holy name of Kṛṣṇa is the highest benediction, above all other benedictions; it is sweeter than the sweetest honey, the eternal fruit of transcendental knowledge of the tree of Vedic scriptures. O best of the Bhargavas! If anyone chants Lord Kṛṣṇa's name just once without offense, whether he chants with faith or indifferently, the holy name immediately liberates him.

ভক্তির প্রকার যত শাস্ত্রে দেখা যায়।
তঁহি মধ্যে নামাশ্রয় শ্রেষ্ঠ বলি' গায়।।
কষ্টেতে অষ্টাঙ্গ যোগে বিষ্ণুস্মৃতি সাধে।
ওষ্ঠস্পন্দনেই শ্রেষ্ঠ কীর্ত্তন বিরাজে।।
অঘচ্ছিৎ স্মরণং বিষ্ণোর্বহ্বায়াসেন সাধ্যতে।
ওষ্ঠস্পন্দনমাত্রেণ কীর্ত্তনন্তু ততো বরম্। (বৈষ্ণব-চিন্তামণিঃ)

bhaktira prakāra yata śāstre dekhā yāya |
taṅhi madhye nāmāśraya śreṣṭha bali gāya ||188||
kaṣṭete aṣṭāṅga yoge viṣṇu-smṛti sādhe |
oṣṭha-spandane-i śreṣṭha kīrtana virāje ||189||
aghacchit-smaraṇaṁ viṣṇor bahv-āyāsena sādhyate |
oṣṭha-spandana-mātreṇa kīrtanaṁ tu tato varam ||190||
[vaiṣṇava-cintāmaṇau, HBV 11.453]

Amongst the different limbs of bhakti, chanting of the holy name is the most efficacious. Astanga-yoga necessitates much arduous exercises in order to remember Viṣṇu.

Although capable of destroying all sins, the remembrance of Lord Viṣṇu is achieved only with extraordinary effort. On the other hand, one may perform kṛṣṇa-kīrtana simply by moving one's lips, and therefore this process is far superior.

দীক্ষাপূর্ব্বক অর্চ্চন যদি শত জন্ম করে।
তাহার জিহ্বায় নিত্য হরিনাম স্ফুরে।।
যেন জন্মশতৈঃ পূর্ব্বং বাসুদেবঃ সমর্চিতঃ।
তন্মুখে হরিনামানি সদা তিষ্ঠন্তি ভারত।। (বৈষ্ণব-চিন্তামণিঃ)

dīkṣā-pūrvaka arcana yadi śata janma kare |
tāhāra jihvāya nitya hari nāma sphure ||191||
yena janma-śataiḥ pūrvaṁ vāsudevaḥ samarcitaḥ |
tan-mukhe hari-nāmāni sadā tiṣṭhanti bhārata ||192||
[vaiṣṇava-cintāmaṇau, HBV 11.454||

O descendant of Bharata, the holy names of Lord Viṣṇu are always vibrating in the mouth of one who has previously worshiped Vāsudeva perfectly for hundreds of lifetimes.

সত্যযুগে বহুকালে যাহা তপোধ্যানে।
যজ্ঞাদি যজিয়া ত্রেতায় যেবা ফল টানে।।
দ্বাপরে অর্চ্চনাঙ্গেতে পায় যেবা ফল।
কলিতে হরিনামে পায় সে সকল।।
ধ্যায়ন্ কৃতে যজন্ যজ্ঞৈস্ত্রেতায়াং দ্বাপরেঽর্চ্চয়ন্।
যদাপ্নোতি তদাপ্নোতি কলৌ সংকীর্ত্ত্য কেশবম্।। (বিষ্ণো পু)

satya-yuge bahu kāle yāhā tapo-dhyāne |
yajñādi yajiyā tretāya yevā phala ṭane ||193||
dvāpare arcanāṅgete pāya yebā phala |
kalite harināme pāya se sakala ||194||
dhyāyan kṛte yajan yajñais tretāyāṁ dvāpare'rcayan |
yad āpnoti tad āpnoti kalau saṅkīrtya keśavam ||195||
[ViP 6.2.17, HBV 11.456||

Whatever is achieved in Satya-yuga by meditation, in Tretā

by offering ritual sacrifices and in Dvāpara by temple worship is achieved in Kali-yuga by chanting the names of Lord Keśava congregationally.

কলিকালে মহাভাগবত বলি তারে।
কীর্ত্তনে যে হরি ভজে এ ভব-সংসারে।।
মহাভাগবতা নিত্যং কলৌ কুর্ব্বন্তি কীর্ত্তনম্।। (স্কন্দ পু)

kali kāle mahābhāgavata bali tāre |
kīrtane ye hari bhaje e bhava saṁsāre ||196||
mahā-bhāgavatā nityaṁ kalau kurvanti kīrtanam ||197||
[skanda, HBV 11.459]

The hallmark of a maha-bhagavata (the most advanced devotee) in kali-yuga is that he chants the holy name constantly. Thus it is very easy to recognize a pure devotee.

চিদাত্মক হরিনাম বারেক উচ্চারে।
শিব-ব্রহ্মা অনন্যতার ফল কহিতে নারে।।
নামোচ্চারণমাহাত্ম্য অদ্ভুত বলি' গায়।
উচ্চারণমাত্রে নর পরমপদ পায়।।
সকৃদুচ্চারয়ন্ত্যেব হরের্নাম চিদাত্মকম্।
ফলং নাস্য ক্ষমো বক্তুং সহস্রবদনো বিধিঃ।।
নামোচ্চারণমাহাত্ম্যং শ্রূয়তে মহদদ্ভুতম্।
যদুচ্চারণমাত্রেণ নরো যায়াৎ পরং পদম্।। (বৃহন্নারদীয়)

cid-ātmaka harināma bāreka uccāre |
śiva brahmā ananyatāra phala kahite nāre ||198||
nāmoccāraṇa-māhātmya adbhuta bali gāya |
uccāraṇa-mātre nara parama pada pāya ||199||
sakṛd uccārayanty eva harer nāma cid-ātmakam |

phalaṁ nāsya kṣamo vaktuṁ sahasra-vadano vidhiḥ ||200||
nāmoccāraṇa-māhātmyaṁ śrūyate mahad adbhutam |
yad uccāraṇa-mātreṇa naro yāyāt paraṁ padam ||201||
(Bṛhan-nāradīya Purāṇa)

The extraordinary result derived from chanting the eternal and transcendentally powerful name of Kṛṣṇa just once cannot be adequately described, even by persons like Lord Śiva or Lord Brahmā. So wondrous are the glories of the holy name that just by chanting it, a person attain the supreme abode.

কৃষ্ণ বলে,—"শুন অর্জ্জুন! বলিব তোমায়।
শ্রদ্ধায় হেলায় জীব মম নাম গায়।।
সেই নাম মম হৃদি সদা বর্ত্তমান।
নামসম ব্রত নাই, নামসম জ্ঞান।।
নামসম ধ্যান নাই নামসম ফল।
নামসম ত্যাগ নাই, নামসম বল।।
নামসম পুণ্য নাই, নামসম গতি।
নামের শক্তিগানে বেদের নাহিক শকতি।।
নামই পরমা মুক্তি, নামই পরমা গতি।
নামই পরমা শান্তি, নামই পরমা স্থিতি।।
নামই পরমা ভক্তি, নামই পরমা মতি।
নামই পরমা প্রীতি, নামই পরমা স্মৃতি।।
জীবের কারণ নাম, নামই জীবের প্রভু।
পরম আরাধ্য নাম, নামই গুরু প্রভু।।"

শ্রদ্ধয়া হেলয়া নাম রটন্তি মম জন্তবঃ।
তেষাং নাম সদা পার্থ বর্ত্ততে হৃদয়ে মম।।
ন নামসদৃশং জ্ঞানং ন নামসদৃশং ব্রতম্।
ন নামসদৃশং ধ্যানং ন নামসদৃশং ফলম্।।
ন নামসদৃশস্ত্যাগো ন নামসদৃশঃ শমঃ।
ন নামসদৃশং পুণ্যং ন নামসদৃশী গতিঃ।।

নামৈব পরমা মুক্তির্নামৈব পরমা গতিঃ।
নামৈব পরমা শান্তির্নামৈব পরমা স্থিতিঃ।।
নামৈব পরমা ভক্তির্নামৈব পরমা মতিঃ।
নামৈব পরমা প্রীতির্নামৈব পরমা স্মৃতিঃ।।
নামৈব কারণং জন্তোর্নামৈব প্রভুরেব চ।
নামৈব পরমারাধ্যং নামৈব পরমো গুরুঃ।। (আদি পুরাণ)

kṛṣṇa bale śuna arjuna baliba tomāya |
śraddhāya helāya jīva mama nāma gāya ||202||
sei nāma mama hṛdi sadā vartamāna |
nāma sama vrata nāi nāma sama jñāna ||203||
nāma sama dhyāna nāi nāma sama phala |
nāma sama tyāga nāi, nāma sama bala ||204||
nāma sama puṇya nāi nāma sama gati |
nāmera śakti gāne vedera nāhika śakati ||205||
nāma-i paramā mukti nāma-i paramā gati |
nāma-i paramā śānti nāma-i paramā sthiti ||206||
nāma-i paramā bhakti nāma-i paramā mati |
nāma-i paramā prīti nāma-i paramā smṛti ||207||
jīvera kāraṇa nāma nāma-i jīvera prabhu |
parama ārādhya nāma nāma-i guru prabhu ||208||

śraddhayā helayā nāma raṭanti mama jantavaḥ |
teṣāṁ nāma sadā pārtha vartate hṛdaye mama ||209 ||
na nāma sadṛśaṁ jñānaṁ na nāma sadṛśaṁ vratam |
na nāma sadṛśaṁ dhyānaṁ na nāma sadṛśaṁ phalam ||210||
na nāma sadṛśas tyāgo na nāma sadṛśaḥ śamaḥ |
na nāma sadṛśaṁ puṇyaṁ na nāma sadṛśī gatiḥ ||211||
nāmaiva paramā muktir nāmaiva paramā gatiḥ |
nāmaiva paramā śāntir nāmaiva paramā sthitiḥ ||212||
nāmaiva paramā bhaktir nāmaiva paramā matiḥ |
nāmaiva paramā prītir nāmaiva paramā smṛtiḥ ||213||
nāmaiva kāraṇaṁ jantor nāmaiva prabhur eva ca |

nāmaiva paramārādhyo nāmaiva paramo guruḥ ||214||
ādi-purāṇa, HBV 11.464-469]

Lord Kṛṣṇa said to Arjuna, 'O Arjuna! Listen attentively. When a living entity chants My name, whether out of devotion or indifference, I never forget this service. It remains always close to My heart.

There is no vow like the holy name, there is no knowledge like the holy name. There is no meditation, there is no benefit, there is no renunciation, there is no strength, there is no pious activity and there is no goal of life like the holy name.

Even the Vedas do not have the power to properly describe the glories of the holy name. Holy name is the highest path to liberation, peace and eternal life.

Holy name is the supreme refuge and the highest form of devotional service. Holy name helps one achieve the highest level of consciousness and the most elevated love of Godhead. Holy name is the best form of remembering the Lord and the holy name has appeared solely for the benefit of the living entity as his Lord and master. Holy name is his supremely worshippable object and his supreme spiritual mentor.

হরিনাম মাহাত্ম্যের কভু নাহি পার।
যে নাম শ্রবণে সদ্য পুক্কশ-উদ্ধার।।
যন্নামসকৃচ্ছ্রবণাৎ পুক্কশোঽপি বিমুচ্যতে সংসারাৎ।
(ভাগবত ৬।১৬।৪৪)

harināma māhātmyera kabhu nāhi pāra |
ye nāma śravaṇe sadā pukkaśa uddhāra ||215||
yan-nāma sakṛc chravaṇāt

pukkaśo'pi vimucyate saṁsārāt ||216||
BhP 6.16.14, HBV 11.486]

There are no limits to the glories of the holy name. Just by hearing the Lord's names even a pukkasa, the lowest of mankind can be delivered. (Bhāg. 6.16.44)

My Lord, it is not impossible for one to be immediately freed from all material contamination by seeing You. Not to speak of seeing You personally, merely by hearing the holy name of Your Lordship only once, even caṇḍālas, men of the lowest class, are freed from all material contamination. Under the circumstances, who will not be freed from material contamination simply by seeing You?

স্বপনে জাগ্রতে যেবা জল্পে কৃষ্ণনাম।
কলিতে সে কৃষ্ণরূপী, কৃষ্ণের বিধান।।
কৃষ্ণ কৃষ্ণেতি কৃষ্ণেতি স্বপন্ জাগ্রদ্ ব্রজংস্তথা।
যো জল্পতি কলৌ নিত্যং কৃষ্ণরূপী ভবেদ্ধি সঃ। (বরাহ পু)

svapane jāgrate yebā jalpe kṛṣṇa nāma |
kalite se kṛṣṇa-rūpī kṛṣṇera vidhāna ||217|
kṛṣṇa kṛṣṇeti kṛṣṇeti svapan jāgrad vrajaṁs tathā |
yo jalpati kalau nityaṁ kṛṣṇa-rūpī bhaved dhi saḥ ||218||
varāha, HBV 11.493||

Whoever continuously chants Kṛṣṇa's name, even in his sleep, can easily realise the name to be a direct manifestation of Kṛṣṇa and achieve Sārūpya liberation. Such person is not influenced by the faults of Kali.

কৃষ্ণ বলি' নিত্য স্মরে সংসার-সাগরে।
জলোত্থিত পদ্ম যেন নরকে উদ্ধরে।।
কৃষ্ণ কৃষ্ণেতি কৃষ্ণেতি যো মাং স্মরতি নিত্যশঃ।
জলং হিত্বা যথা পদ্মং নরকাদুদ্ধরাম্যহম্।। (নরসিংহ পুরাণ)

kṛṣṇa bali nitya smare saṁsāra sāgare |
jalotthita padma yena narake uddhare ||219||
kṛṣṇa kṛṣṇeti kṛṣṇeti yo māṁ smarati nityaśaḥ |
jalaṁ bhittvā yathā padmaṁ narakād uddharāmy aham ||220||
nārasiṁhe, HBV 11.496]

One who chants Kṛṣṇa's name and constantly remembers Him, even though fallen in this ocean of birth and death, is like the lotus which is born in the water but is untouched by it. It's a transcendental position. Such person is quickly rescued by the Lord and he himself becomes capable of delivering the residents of the hellish planets. (Nṛsiṁha Purāṇa)

কৃষ্ণনাম সর্ব্বমুখ্য জীবের আশ্রয়।
অশেষ পাপ হরে, সদ্য পাপমুক্তিকর।।
নাম্নাং মুখ্যতরং নাম কৃষ্ণাখ্যং মে পরন্তপ।
প্রায়শ্চিত্তমশেষাণাং পাপানাং মোচনং পরম্।। (প্রভাসখণ্ড)

kṛṣṇa-nāma sarva mukhya jīvera āśraya |
aśeṣa pāpa hare sadya pāpa mukti kara ||221||
nāmnāṁ mukhyataraṁ nāma kṛṣṇākhyaṁ me parantapa |
prāyaścittam aśeṣāṇāṁ pāpānāṁ mocakaṁ param ||222||
[prabhāsa-purāṇe, HBV 11.498]

The holy name is the prime and most secure shelter for the living entity. The holy name destroys his countless sinful reactions and liberates him.

নাম—চিন্তামণি, কৃষ্ণ, চৈতন্য-স্বরূপ।
পূর্ণ, শুদ্ধ, নিত্যমুক্ত, নামনামী একরূপ।।
নাম চিন্তামণিঃ কৃষ্ণশ্চৈতন্যরসবিগ্রহঃ।
পূর্ণঃ শুদ্ধো নিত্যমুক্তোঽভিন্নত্বাৎ নামনামিনোঃ।।
(ভক্তিরসামৃতসিন্ধু পূ বি ২।১০৮)

nāma cintāmaṇi kṛṣṇa caitanya svarūpa |
pūrṇa śuddha nitya mukta nāma nāmī eka rūpa ||223||
nāma cintāmaṇiḥ kṛṣṇaś caitanyarasavigrahaḥ |
pūrṇaḥ śuddho nityamukto bhinnatvān nāmanāminoḥ ||224||
[HBV 11.503]

The holy name of Kṛṣna is transcendentally blissful. It bestows all spiritual benedictions, for it is Kṛṣna Himself, the reservoir of all pleasure. Kṛṣṇa's name is complete, and it is the form of all transcendental mellows. It is not a material name under any condition, and it is no less powerful than Kṛṣṇa Himself. Since Kṛṣṇa's name is not contaminated by the material qualities, there is no question of its being involved with māyā. Kṛṣṇa's name is always liberated and spiritual; it is never conditioned by the laws of material nature. This is because the name of Kṛṣṇa and Kṛṣṇa Himself are identical.

বিষ্ণুনাম বিষ্ণুশক্তি যেই জন জানে।
সুমতি প্রার্থনা করে অপ্রাকৃত জ্ঞানে।।
ওঁ আঽস্য জানন্তো নাম চিদ্বিবক্তন্।
মহস্তে বিষ্ণো সুমতিং ভজামহে ওঁ তৎ সৎ।।
(ঋগ্বেদ ১ম মণ্ডল, ১৫৬ সূক্ত, ৩ ঋক্)

viṣṇu nāma viṣṇu śakti yei jana jāne |
sumati prārthanā kare aprākṛta jñāne ||225||

oṁ āsya jānanto nāma cid viviktan
mahas te viṣṇo sumatiṁ bhajāmahe ||226||
ṛkveda 1.156.3, HBV 11.510]

One who philosophically understands that the Lord's holy name and His potencies are one and the same can properly approach and worship the Lord with transcendental knowledge and choice prayers. (Rg Veda 1.56.3)

স্থানেশ্বরী কৃষ্ণদাস যোড় করি' কর।
বলে,—"প্রভু, এক বস্তু প্রার্থনা হামার।।
এরূপ মাহাত্ম্য নামের শুনিনু শ্রবণে।
সর্ব্বত্র সমান ফল নাহি হোয় কেনে।।"
প্রভু বলে,—"শ্রদ্ধা বিশ্বাস সকলের মূল।
বিশ্বাস-অভাবে কেহ্ নাহি লভে ফল।।"
প্রভু বলে,—"অন্তর্য্যামী নাম ভগবান্।
বিশ্বাসানুসারে ফল করেন প্রদান।।
নামের মহিমা পূর্ণ বিশ্বাস না করে।
নামের ফল নাহি পায়, নাম-অপরাধে মরে।।
অর্থবাদ করে ফলে বিশ্বাস ত্যজিয়া।
ফল নাহি পায়, থাকে নরকে পড়িয়া।।"
অর্থবাদং হরের্নাম্নি সম্ভাবয়তি যো নরঃ।
স পাপিষ্ঠো মনুষ্যাণাং নিরয়ে পততি স্ফুটম্।।
(কাত্যায়নী সংহিতা)

sthāneśvarī kṛṣṇa-dāsa yoḍa kari kara |
bale prabhu eka vastu prārthanā hāmāra ||227||
e rūpa māhātmya nāmera śuninu śravaṇe |
sarvatra samāna phala nāhi hoya kene ||228||
prabhu bale—śraddhā viśvāsa sakalera mūla |
viśvāsa abhāve keha nāhi labhe phala ||229||

prabhu bale—antaryāmī nāma bhagavān |
viśvāsānusāre phala karena pradāna ||230||
nāmera mahimā pūrṇa viśvāsa nā kare |
nāmera phala nāhi pāya nāma aparādhe mare ||231||
artha vāda kare phale viśvāsa tyajiyā |
phala nāhi pāya thāke narake paḍiyā ||232||
artha-vādaṁ harer nāmni sambhāvayati yo naraḥ |
sa pāpiṣṭho manuṣyāṇāṁ niraye patanti sphuṭam ||233||
[kātyāyana-saṁhitā, HBV 11.514||

Śrī Kṛṣṇadāsa, a resident of Puri, then enquired from Lord Caitanya with folded hands: Dear Lord, I have a doubt which I place before Your lotus feet: after having heard the wonderful glories of the holy name, I wonder why the holy name does not always give everyone the same result.

The Lord replied, sraddhā (faith) is the foundation of everything in spiritual life. Some people do not get immediate results from chanting due to their lack of faith. The holy name is the Supreme Lord Himself, residing in everyone's heart as the Supersoul and He offers success in chanting proportionate to his faith. Persons, even after hearing the holy name's glories, do not have sufficient faith in the holy name or in the chanting process cannot make spiritual progress. Instead they glide down towards nescience, committing offenses against the holy name.

They misinterpret the glories and transcendental nature of the holy name, and due to this offense they suffer hellish existence.

যন্নামকীর্ত্তনফলং বিবিধং নিশম্য
ন শ্রদ্দধাতি মনুতে যদুতার্থবাদম্।
যো মানুষস্তমিহ দুঃখচয়ে ক্ষিপামি
সংসার-ঘোর-বিবিধার্ত্তিনিপীড়িতাঙ্গম্।। (ব্রহ্মসংহিতা)

yan-nāma-kīrtana-phalaṁ vividhaṁ niśamya
na śraddadhāti manute yad utārtha-vādam |
yo mānuṣas tam iha duḥkha-caye kṣipāmi
saṁsāra-ghora-vividhārti-nipīḍitāṅgam ||234||
[brahma-saṁhitā HBV 11.515]

That person who even after hearing about the wonderful results of chanting harināma refuses to develop sincere śraddhā in harināma and, on the contrary, expostulates that such elucidations of the potency of harināma are inflated panegyrics is hurled by Me into the deep gloom of material nescience after being dragged through excruciating suffering.

The Mysteries of the Holy Name

(nāma rahasya paṭala)

একদা গৌরাঙ্গচাঁদ চন্দ্রালোক পাইয়া।
সমুদ্রের তীরে আইল ভক্তবৃন্দ লঞা।।
হরিদাস-সমাজের উপকণ্ঠে বসি'।
সর্ব্ব বৈষ্ণবের প্রতি বলে গৌরশশী।।

ekadā gaurāṅga cāṅda candrāloka pāiyā |
samudrera tīre āila bhakta vṛnda lañā ||1||
hari dāsa samājera upakaṇṭha basi |
sarva vaiṣṇavera prati bale gaura śaśī ||2||

Once on a bright moonlit night, Lord Caitanya, the Moon of Navadvipa came on the ocean beach along with His associates. He sat down in the midst of His associates like an iridescent moon, and began to speak to the assembly.

শ্রীনামই একমাত্র ও শ্রেষ্ঠ সাধন

"শুন হে ভকতবৃন্দ! কলিকালের ধর্ম্ম।
শ্রীকৃষ্ণকীর্ত্তন বিনা আর নাহি কর্ম্ম।।
কর্ম্ম-জ্ঞান-যোগ-ধ্যান দুর্ব্বল সাধন।
অপ্রাকৃত সম্পত্তি লাভের নহে ক্রম।।

śrī nāma-i eka mātra o śreṣṭha sādhan:

śuna he bhakata vṛnda kali kālera dharma |

śrī kṛṣṇa kīrtana vinā āra nāhi karma ||3||
karma jñāna yoga dhyāna durbala sādhana |
aprākṛta sampatti lābhera nahe krama ||4||

The holy name is the best and only means to perfection:

He said, My dear devotees! In Kali-yuga there is no spiritual activity and religious practice to surpass congregational chanting of Lord Kṛṣṇa's name. Fruitive activities, cultivation of knowledge, yoga or meditation are extremely ineffectual processes for spiritual realization. They cannot help one reach the transcendental platform and realize the Absolute Truth.

ধর্ম্ম, ব্রত, ত্যাগ, হোম সকলই প্রাকৃত।
অপ্রাকৃততত্ত্বলাভে নাহি করে হিত।।
কৃষ্ণনাম উচ্চারণে, স্মরণে, শ্রবণে।
অপ্রাকৃতসিদ্ধি হয়, বলে শ্রুতিগণে।।
শ্রীনামরহস্য সর্ব্বশাস্ত্রেতে দেখিবা।
নাম-উচ্চারণমাত্র চিৎসুখ লভিবা।।

dharma vrata tyāga homa sakala-i prākṛta |
aprākṛta tattva lābhe nāhi kare hita ||5||
kṛṣṇa nāma uccāraṇe smaraṇe śravaṇe |
aprākṛta siddhi haya bale śruti gaṇe ||6||
śrī nāma rahasya sarva śāstrete dekhibā |
nāma uccāraṇa mātra cit sukha labhibā ||7||

Prescribed religious duties, penances, renunciation and sacrifices are all mundane activities. Hence, they cannot help one reach the absolute plane—the spiritual world. Vedas declare that the highest summit of spiritual perfection can be achieved through chanting, hearing and remembering Kṛṣṇa's name. All scriptures reveal the esoteric truth about the holy name and one experiences transcendental bliss immediately upon chanting the holy name.

পদ্মপুরাণ স্বর্গখণ্ড ১৮ অধ্যায়, নামরহস্যপটলং যথা
শ্রীশৌনক উবাচ
নামোচ্চারণমাহাত্ম্যং শ্রূয়তে মহদদ্ভুতম্
যদুচ্চারণমাত্রেণ নরো যায়াৎ পরং পদম্
তদ্বদস্বাধুনা সুত বিধানং নামকীর্ত্তনে
শৃণু শোণক বক্ষ্যাম সংবাদং মোক্ষসাধনম্।
নারদঃ পৃষ্টবান্ পূর্ব্বং কুমারং তদ্বদামি তে।।
একদা যমুনাতীরে নিবিষ্টং শান্তমানসম্।
সনৎকুমারং পপ্রচ্ছ নারদো রচিতাঞ্জলিঃ।
শ্রুত্বা নানাবিধান্ ধর্ম্মান্ ধর্ম্মব্যতিকরাংস্তথা।।
শ্রীনারদ উবাচ
যোঽসৌ ভগবতা প্রোক্তো ধর্ম্মব্যতিকরো নৃণাম্।
কথং তস্য বিনাশঃ স্যাদুচ্যতাং ভগবৎপ্রিয়।।

padma-purāṇe svarga-khaṇḍa 18 adhyāya, nāma-rahasya-paṭalaṁ, yathā:
śrī-śaunaka uvāca—
nāmoccāraṇa-māhātmyaṁ śrūyate mahad-adbhutam |
yad uccāraṇa-mātreṇa naro yāyāt paraṁ padam |
tadvad asvādhunā sūta vidhānaṁ nāma-kīrtane ||8||
śrī-sūta uvāca—
śṛṇu śaunaka vakṣyāmi saṁvādaṁ mokṣa-sādhanam |
nāradaḥ pṛṣṭavān pūrvaṁ kumāraṁ tad vadāmi te ||9||
ekadā yamunā-tīre niviṣṭaṁ śānta-mānasam |
sanat-kumāraṁ papraccha nārado racitāñjaliḥ
śrutvā nānā-vidhān dharmān dharma-vyatikarāṁs tathā ||10||
śrī-nārada uvāca—
yo'sau bhagavatā prokto dharma-vyatikaro nṛṇām |

kathaṁ tasya vināśaḥ syād ucyatāṁ bhagavat-priya ||11||

These Purāṇic slokas are explained by Lord Chaitanya in the following verses.

এই পটলের অর্থ কিছু বিশেষ করিয়া।
বলি স্বরূপ রামানন্দ শুন মন দিয়া।।

ei paṭalera artha kichu viśeṣa kariyā |
bali svarūpa rāmānanda śuna mana diyā ||12||

The Supreme Lord Śrī Caitanya Mahāprabhu continued, I will explain in some detail the meaning of these slokas. O Svarūpa Dāmodara and Rāmānanda, listen carefully with attention!

শ্রীনামকীর্ত্তন কি?—'উচ্চারণ'

'উচ্চারণ'-শব্দে বুঝ শ্রীনামকীর্ত্তন।
'করে' বা 'মালায়' সংখ্যা করে ভক্তগণ।।
সংখ্যা ছাড়ি' অসংখ্য নাম কভু কভু হয়।
'উচ্চারণ'-শব্দে এসব জানহ নিশ্চয়।।

śrī-nāma-kīrtana ki? 'uccāraṇa'

uccāraṇa śabde bujha śrī nāma kīrtana |
kare vā mālāya saṅkhyā kare bhakta gaṇa ||13||
saṅkhyā chāḍi asaṅkhya nāma kabhu kabhu haya |
uccāraṇa śabde e saba jānaha niścaya ||14||

Uccarana defined:

The meaning of the word uccarana in this context is to chant or sing the holy name loudly or audibly. The devotees generally keep a count either on their fingers or on the beads. Many chant extra or sing in kīrtana which is in addition to the prescribed number. Therefore basically, audible chanting of the holy name is referred to as uccarana.

জপ ও কীর্ত্তন

লঘূচ্চারে 'জপ' হয়, উচ্চারে কীর্ত্তন।
স্মরণ কীর্ত্তনে সব হয় ত' গণন।।
কি প্রকারে নাম কৈলে সুকীর্ত্তন হয়।
শ্রীনামকীর্ত্তনে তাহা বিধান নিশ্চয়।।

japa o kīrtana

laghūccāre japa haya uccāre kīrtana |
smaraṇa kīrtane saba haya ta gaṇana ||15||
ki prakāre nāma kaile sukīrtana haya |
śrī nāma kīrtane tāhā vidhāna niścaya ||16||

Japa and kīrtana defined:

When the chanting is soft and barely audible, it is known as japa and when the chanting is loud and clear, it is known as kirtana. Both of these are counted as smaraṇa or remembrance. It is imperative for everyone to know how to properly chant the holy name and thereby derive the utmost benefit from it.

কীর্ত্তন সর্ব্বথা ও সর্ব্বদা কর্ত্তব্য

শ্রীনামকীর্ত্তন হয় জীবের নিত্যধর্ম্ম।
জগতে বৈকুণ্ঠে জীবের এই মুখ্য কর্ম্ম।।
মায়াবদ্ধ জীবের এই মোক্ষ সাধন হয়।
মুক্তজীবের পক্ষে তাহা সাধ্যাবধি রয়।।

kīrtana sarvathā o sarvadā kartavya

śrī nāma kīrtana haya jīvera nitya dharma |
jagate vaikuṇṭhe jīvera ei mukhya karma ||17||
māyā baddha jīvera ei mokṣa sādhana haya |
mukta jīvera pakṣe tāhā sādhyāvadhi raya ||18||

Perform kīrtana always and everywhere:

Chanting the holy name is the eternal religion of the living entity. It is his prime duty, both in the material world and in the spiritual world. It is his foremost activity, both in his conditional life as well as liberated life.

In the conditional state, chanting is the means to achieve liberation, and in the liberated state, chanting remains an eternal, integral part of his service to the Supreme Lord.

ভক্তিহীন শুভকার্য্য ত্যজ্য

ধর্ম্মশাস্ত্র-উক্ত ভক্তিহীন ধর্ম্ম যত।
ভক্ত্যুদ্দেশ বিনা আর যত প্রকার ব্রত।।
ভক্ত্যুত্থিত বিরাগ ব্যতীত যত ত্যাগ।
ভক্তি-প্রতিকূল যজ্ঞ প্রাকৃত বিভাগ।।
এই সব শুভকর্ম্ম সম্বন্ধ বিচারে।
ভক্তি-অনুকূল বলি' শাস্ত্রেতে প্রচারে।।

bhakti hīna śubha kārya tyajya

dharma śāstra ukta bhakti hīna dharma yata |
bhakty-uddeśa vinā āra yata prakāra vrata ||19||
bhakty-utthita virāga vyatīta yata tyāga |
bhakti pratikūla yajña prākṛta vibhāga ||20||
ei saba śubha karma sambandha vicāre |
bhakti anukūla bali śāstrete pracāre ||21||

Activities devoid of bhakti are to be rejected:

All non-devotional rituals mentioned in the religious scriptures, all kinds of sacred vows that do not aim at developing devotional service, all types of dry renunciation and all type of sacrifice that are unfavorable for devotional service, all these are considered pious activities. But these very activities, when performed in relationship to devotional service, become favourable spiritual activities and they constitute bhakti. This is the verdict of the revealed scriptures.

কলিকালে সেই সব জড়ধর্ম্ম হইল।
ভক্তি-আনুকূল্য ত্যজি' ধর্ম্ম নষ্ট ভেল।
অতএব কলিকালে নামসংকীর্ত্তন।
বিনা আর ধর্ম্ম নাই শুন ভক্তগণ।।
সে ধর্ম্মের ব্যতিকর যাহাই দেখিবে।
তাহাই বর্জ্জিবে যত্নে ভক্তির প্রভাবে।।

kali kāle sei saba jaḍa dharma ha-ila |
bhakti ānukūlya tyaji dharma naṣṭa bhela ||22||
ataeva kali kāle nāma saṅkīrtana |
vinā āra dharma nāi śuna bhakta gaṇa ||23||
se dharmera vyatikara yāhāi dekhibe |
tāhāi varjibe yatne bhaktira prabhāve ||24||

But in Kali-yuga, all these activities have lost spiritual potency and have turned into mundane, materialistic activities. These activities are no more favorable to devotional service.

Therefore, O devotees! Hear with attention that in Kali-yuga, there is no other religion than the congregational chanting of the holy name. Other religious practices that exist outside of this chanting process should be strictly avoided.

শ্রীসনৎকুমার উবাচ
শৃণু নারদ গোবিন্দপ্রিয় গোবিন্দধর্ম্মবিৎ।
যৎ পৃষ্টং লোকনির্ম্মুক্তিকারণং তমসঃ পরম্ ।।

śrī-sanatkumāra uvāca

śṛṇu nārada govinda-priya govinda-dharma-vit |
yat pṛṣṭaṁ loka-nirmukti-kāraṇaṁ tamasaḥ param ||4||25||

This sloka is explained by Lord Chaitanya in the following verses.

তুমি ত' নারদ শ্রীগোবিন্দধর্ম্মবেত্তা।
গোবিন্দের প্রিয়, মায়াবন্ধনের ছেত্তা ।।
লোকনির্ম্মুক্তির হেতু জিজ্ঞাসা তোমার।
তব প্রশ্নোত্তরে জীব হবে তমঃ পার ।।
কলিতে সকল ধর্ম্মাধর্ম্ম তমোময়।
নামধর্ম্ম বিনা জীবের সংসার নহে ক্ষয় ।।

tumi ta nārada śrī-govinda-dharma-vettā |
govindera priya māyā bandhanera chettā ||26||
loka nirmuktira hetu jijñāsā tomāra |
tava praśnottare jīva habe tamaḥ pāra ||27||
kalite sakala dharmādharma tamo-maya |
nāma dharma vinā jīvera saṁsāra nahe kṣaya ||28||

O Nārada! You are well-versed in the science of devotional service and you are very dear to Kṛṣṇa. You can cut asunder the chains of material entanglement that keep the living entities bound to this world.

Your question is glorious as it is aimed at liberating the people in general. By hearing about your inquiry and its answer, the living entities will cross beyond this insurmountable ocean of nescience.

In Kali-yuga all things, religious and irreligious, are covered by the mode of ignorance. Therefore, the only path of liberation open to the living beings is the chanting of the holy name.

অতএব নামে সর্ব্বপাপক্ষয়

সর্ব্বাচারবিবর্জ্জিতাঃ শঠধিয়ো ব্রাত্যা জগদ্বঞ্চকাঃ
দম্ভাহঙ্কৃতিপানপৈশুন্যপরাঃ পাপাশ্চ যে নিষ্ঠুরাঃ।
যে চান্যে ধনদারপুত্রনিরতাঃ সর্ব্বেঽধমাস্তেঽপি হি।
শ্রীগোবিন্দপদারবিন্দশরণাঃ শুদ্ধাঃ ভবন্তি দ্বিজ।। ৫।।

ataeva nāme sarva pāpa kṣaya

sarvācāra-vivarjitāḥ śaṭha-dhiyo vrātyā jagad-vañcakāḥ
dambhāhaṅkṛti-pāna-paiśunya-parāḥ pāpāś ca ye niṣṭhurāḥ |
ye cānye dhana-dāra-putra-niratāḥ sarve'dhamās te'pi hi
śrī-govinda-padāravinda-śaraṇāḥ śuddhāḥ bhavanti dvija
||5||29||

The holy name alone can purify from all sinful reactions:

'One who takes shelter of Lord Govinda's lotus feet, all his sins are eradicated by chanting of the holy name. He becomes completely purified even though he may be an abominable wretch, a big liar and a cheat, arrogant and cruel, always given to sinful ways and a grossly materialistic person attached to wife, children and wealth.

শ্রীগোবিন্দপদারবিন্দে শরণ যে লয়।
তা'র সর্ব্বপাপ নামে নিশ্চয় হয় ক্ষয়।।
কৃষ্ণনাম লয়ে কাঁদে, নিজ দোষ বলে।
অতি শীঘ্র তা'র পাপ যায় ভক্তিবলে।।

śrī-govinda-padāravinda śaraṇa ye laya |
tāra sarva-pāpa nāme niścaya haya kṣaya ||30||
kṛṣṇa-nāma laye kāṅde nija doṣa bale |
ati śīghra tāra pāpa yāya bhakti bale ||31||

All sinful activities of a person who takes shelter of the lotus feet of Govinda, certainly becomes vanquished by the chanting of the holy name.

If one chants Lord Kṛṣṇa's name, crying regretfully while sincerely repenting for his past misdeeds, all his sins are washed away by the potency of such devotional service.

কর্ম্মপ্রায়শ্চিত্তে বাসনা নষ্ট হয় না

কর্ম্মজ্ঞান-প্রায়শ্চিত্তে তা'র কিবা ফল।
সে ফল দুর্ব্বল অতি, তা'র নাহি বল।।
এক কৃষ্ণনামে পাপীর যত পাপক্ষয়।
বহু জন্মে সেই পাপী করিতে নারয়।।
হেন পাপ স্মার্ত্তশাস্ত্রে না আছে বর্ণন।
এক কৃষ্ণনামে যাহা না হয় খণ্ডন।।
তবে কেন স্মার্ত্তলোক প্রায়শ্চিত্ত করে ?
সুকৃতি-অভাবে তা'র কর্ম্মে মতি হরে।।
কর্ম্ম-প্রায়শ্চিত্তে কভু বাসনা না যায়।
জ্ঞানপ্রায়শ্চিত্তে শোধে বাসনা হিয়ায়।।

বাসনার মূল অবিদ্যা ভক্তিতে বিনষ্ট হয়

পুনঃ কিছুদিনে সে বাসনা হয় স্থূল।

ভক্তিতে অবিদ্যা যায় বাসনার মূল ।।
যে জন গোবিন্দপদে লইয়া শরণ ।
নাম লয় কাকুভরে করয় রোদন ।।
তা'র পক্ষে শ্রীমুখের বাক্য সুমধুর ।
জীবের মঙ্গল, গীতায় দেখহ প্রচুর ।।

karma-prāyaścitta vāsanā naṣṭa haya nā

karma jñāna prāyaścitte tāra kibā phala |
se phala durbala ati tāra nāhi bala ||32||
eka kṛṣṇa nāme pāpīra yata pāpa kṣaya |
bahu janme sei pāpī karite nāraya ||33||
hena pāpa smārta śāstre nā āche varṇana |
eka kṛṣṇa nāme yāhā nā haya khaṇḍana ||34||
tabe kena smārta loka prāyaścitta kare |
sukṛti abhāve tāra karme mati hare ||35||
karma prāyaścitte kabhu vāsanā nā yāya |
jñāna prāyaścitte śodhe vāsanā hiyāya ||36||

vāsanāra mūla avidyā bhaktite vinaṣṭa haya

punaḥ kichu dine se vāsanā haya sthūla |
bhaktite avidyā yāya vāsanāra mūla ||37||
ye jana govinda pade laiyā śaraṇa |
nāma laya kāku bhare karaya rodana ||38||
tāra pakṣe śrī mukhera vākya sumadhura |
jīvera maṅgala gītāya dekhaha pracura ||39||

Ritualistic atonement cannot destroy material desires and purify the heart:

Atonement with ritualistic activities and atonement with speculative knowledge are very weak processes. Their impact is too feeble to destroy sinful reactions and purify the heart. On the other hand, Krsna's holy name, chanted even once, can destroy more sins than an ardent sinner can possibly commit in many lifetimes.

Vedic scriptures that deal with regulative principles and ritualistic performances, enlist many types of sinful activities. All these sinful activities can be counteracted easily by chanting of Krsna's name just once.

Then the question may be raised as to why do these followers of smārta system undergo ritualistic atonement and not just take shelter of Krsna's name? This is because they lack sufficient piety or good fortune and their intelligence is polluted.

The desire to commit sinful activities is never destroyed by performing ritualistic atonement. By performing atonement with cultivation of knowledge such desire may be temporarily curbed, but soon, in no time it raises its ugly head again and make the person commit sinful activities again. But Devotional service roots out the ignorance within the heart which is the root cause of all sinful desires.

Souls who surrender at Govinda's lotus feet, cry piteously while chanting His name. Such souls are glorified in Bhagavad-gita, which contains instructions by the Lord Himself for the benefit of all living entities.

The blessed Lord says:

শ্রীগীতা

"সর্ব্বধর্ম্মান্ পরিত্যজ্য মামেকং শরণং ব্রজ।
অহং ত্বাং সর্ব্বপাপেভ্যো মোক্ষয়িষ্যামি মা শুচঃ।।
অপি চেৎ সুদুরাচারো ভজতে মামনন্যভাক্।
সাধুরেব স মন্তব্যঃ সম্যগ্ব্যবসিতো হি সঃ।।
ক্ষিপ্রং ভবতি ধর্ম্মাত্মা শশ্বচ্ছান্তিং নিগচ্ছতি।
কৌন্তেয় প্রতিজানীহি ন মে ভক্তঃ প্রণশ্যতি।।"

śrī gītā

sarva-dharmān parityajya mām ekaṁ śaraṇaṁ vraja |
ahaṁ tvāṁ sarva-pāpebhyo mokṣayiṣyāmi mā śucaḥ ||40||

Abandon all varieties of religion and just surrender unto Me. I shall deliver you from all sinful reaction. Do not fear. (Bg. 18.66).

api cet sudurācāro bhajate mām ananya-bhāk |
sādhur eva sa mantavyaḥ samyag vyavasito hi saḥ ||41||

Even if one commits the most abominable actions, if he is engaged in devotional service, he is to be considered saintly because he is properly situated. (Bg. 9.30).

kṣipraṁ bhavati dharmātmā śāśvac-chāntiṁ nigacchati |
kaunteya pratijāhīhi na me bhaktaḥ praṇaśyati ||42||

He quickly becomes righteous and attains lasting peace. O son of Kunti, declare it boldly that My devotee never perishes. (Bg. 9.31).

অতএব নামের ফল

অতএব কর্ম্মাঙ্গ প্রায়শ্চিত্তাদি পরিহরি'।
বুদ্ধিমান্ জন ভজে প্রাণেশ্বর হরি।।

ataeva nāmera phala

ataeva karmāṅga prāyaścittādi parihari'
buddhimān jana bhaje prāṇeśvara hari ||43||

The results of chanting

Therefore, one should give up the practices of ritualistic

atonement and other such fruitive activities. A truly intelligent person worships the Supreme Lord Hari, knowing Him to be the dearmost Lord of his heart.

"তমপি দেবকরং করুণাকরং
স্থাবর-জঙ্গম-মুক্তিকরং পরম্।
অতিচরন্ত্যপরাধপরা জনা য
ইহ তানবতিধ্রুবনাম হি।।" ৬।।

tam api deva-karaṁ karuṇākaraṁ
sthāvara-jaṅgama-mukti-karaṁ param |
aticaranty aparādha-parā janā
ya iha tānavati dhruva-nāma hi ||44||

This Sanskrit verse is explained by the Lord in the following Bengali verses

কৃষ্ণনাম দয়াময় কৃষ্ণতেজোময়।
স্থাবর-জঙ্গম-মুক্তিদাতা সুনিশ্চয়।।
নাম-অপরাধী তাহে করে অপরাধ।
অতিচার আসি' নাম-ধর্ম্মে করে বাধ।।
সেই মহা-অপরাধীর দোষ, নামে হয় ক্ষয়।
নাম বিনা জীববন্ধু জগতে না হয়।।

kṛṣṇa-nāma dayāmaya kṛṣṇa-tejo-maya |
sthāvara jaṅgama mukti dātā suniścaya ||45||
nāma aparādhī tāhe kare aparādha |
aticāra āsi nāma dharme kare bādha ||46||
sei mahā aparādhīra doṣa nāme haya kṣaya |
nāma vinā jīva bandhu jagate nā haya ||47||

The holy name of Kṛṣṇa is compassionate and invested with Kṛṣṇa's full potencies. It can easily liberate all moving and non-moving beings. One who chants but commits offenses against the holy name, is burdened with sins. This causes upheavals in his spiritual life. The only way this can be counteracted is by taking complete shelter of the holy name. There is no greater well-wishing friend in the entire world other than the holy name of the Lord.

শ্রীনারদ উবাচ

"কে তেঽপরাধা বিপ্রেন্দ্র নাম্নো ভগবতঃ কৃতা।
বিনিঘ্নন্তি নৃণাং কৃত্যং প্রাকৃতং হ্যানয়ন্তি চ।।"

śrī-nārada uvāca—
ke te'parādhā viprendra nāmno bhagavataḥ kṛtā |
vinighnanti nṛṇāṁ kṛtyaṁ prākṛtaṁ hy ānayanti ca ||48||

This is explained in the following verses.

নামাপরাধ

ওহে গুরু সনৎকুমার কৃপা করি' বল।
নামে অপরাধ যত প্রকার সকল।।
নামরূপ মহাকৃত্য জীবের নিশ্চয়।
সেই কৃত্য যাহে সাধকের নষ্ট নয়।।
নামকে প্রাকৃত করি' সাধন করাঞা।
সামান্য প্রাকৃত ফলে দেয় ফেলাইয়া।।

nāmāparādha

ohe guru sanat-kumāra kṛpā kari' bala |
nāme aparādha yata prakāra sakala ||49||
nāma rūpa mahā kṛtya jīvera niścaya |
sei kṛtya yāhe sādhakera naṣṭa naya ||50||

nāmake prākṛta kari sādhana karāñā |
sāmānya prākṛta phale deya phelāiyā ||51||

O Sanatkumāra, my dear spiritual master, kindly enumerate the different offenses to the holy name. Chanting the holy name is the prime duty and religious practice for the living entity and his ultimate shelter. Care must be taken that the aspiring devotee does not fall into māyā's trap due to offenses. Offenses can misguide the devotee into believing that chanting is a mundane activity. In this way, he ends up with meagre material benefits instead of the real benediction.

শ্রীসনৎকুমার উবাচ

"সতাং নিন্দা নাম্নঃ পরমপরাধং বিতনুতে
যতঃ খ্যাতিং যাতং কথমুসহতে তদ্বিগর্হাম্।"
"শিবস্য শ্রীবিষ্ণোর্য ইহ গুণনামাদিসকলং
ধিয়াভিন্নং পশ্যেৎ স খলু হরিনামাহিতকরঃ।।" ৮।।

śrī-sanatkumāra uvāca—
satāṁ nindā nāmnaḥ paramam aparādhaṁ vitanute
yataḥ khyātiṁ yātaṁ katham u sahate tadvigarhām |
śivasya śrīviṣṇor ya iha guṇanāmādisakalaṁ
dhiyā bhinnaṁ paśyet sa khalu harināmāhitakaraḥ ||8||52||

This verse will be explained in the following verses.

নামাপরাধ হইতে মুক্তি

দশটী নামাপরাধ ভিন্ন ভিন্ন করি'।
বুঝিয়া লইলে নাম-অপরাধে তরি।।
এই শ্লোকে দুই অপরাধের বিচার।
করিয়া করহ শুদ্ধ নামের আচার।।

nāmāparādha haite mukti

daśa-ṭī nāmāparādha bhinna bhinna kari |
bujhiyā laile nāma aparādha tari ||53||
ei śloke dui aparādhera vicāra |
kariyā karaha śuddha nāmera ācāra ||54||

Try to understand each of the ten offenses to the holy name individually. Then you can avoid them. This sloka analyzes two offenses. Avoid them and try to chant purely.

সাধুনিন্দা

একান্ত-নামেতে আশ্রয় আছে যাঁর।
সাধুপদবাচ্য তেঁহ তারেন সংসার।।
জড়কর্ম্মজ্ঞানচেষ্টা ছাড়ি' সেই জন।
শুদ্ধভক্তিভাবে নাম করেন উচ্চারণ।।
নামের প্রচার একা তাঁহা হৈতে হয়।
তাঁর নিন্দা কৃষ্ণনাম কভু না সহয়।।
সে সাধুর নিন্দা, তাঁতে, লঘু-বুদ্ধি যার।
বড় অপরাধ নামে নিশ্চয় তাহার।।
যত্নে এই অপরাধ করিয়া বর্জ্জন।
সেই সাধু-সঙ্গ-বলে করহ ভজন।।

sādhu nindā

ekānta nāmete āśraya āche yāṅra |
sādhu pada vācya teṅha tārena saṁsāra ||55||
jaḍa karma jñāna ceṣṭā chāḍi sei jana |
śuddha bhakti bhāve nāma karena uccāraṇa ||56||
nāmera pracāra ekā tāṅhā haite haya |
tāṅra nindā kṛṣṇa nāma kabhu nā sahaya ||57||
se sādhura nindā tāṅte laghu buddhi yāra |

baḍa aparādha nāme niścaya tāhāra ||58||
yatne ei aparādha kariyā varjana |
sei sādhu saṅga bale karaha bhajana ||59||

According to the verdict of the saintly devotees, a person who takes complete shelter of the holy name, can deliver the whole universe. He gives up all endeavours for cultivation of material knowledge and fruitive activities and dedicates himself to exclusively chant the holy name in pure Krishna consciousness.

Such an exalted soul is eligible to propagate the glories of the holy name. The holy name of Krishna never tolerates criticism of such a saintly devotee and his minimisation in any way is never taken lightly by Krishna.

Therefore meticulously refrain from committing this grave offense and aspire for his saintly association. Execute devotional service under his benign shelter.

শ্রীনাম-নামী একতত্ত্ব

মঙ্গলস্বরূপ বিষ্ণু পরতত্ত্ব হরি।
অপ্রাকৃত স্বরূপেতে শ্রীব্রজবিহারী।।
তাঁ'র নাম-রূপ-গুণ-লীলা অপ্রাকৃত।
তাঁহার স্বরূপ হৈতে ভিন্ন নহে তত্ত্ব।।
নাম নামী এক তত্ত্ব অপ্রাকৃত ধর্ম্ম।
এ জড়জগতে তা'র নাহি আছে মর্ম্ম।।
এই শুদ্ধজ্ঞানলাভ ভক্তিবলে হয়।
তর্কে বহু দূর ইহা জানিহ নিশ্চয়।।
নিজ শুদ্ধসাধন, আর সাধুগুরুবল।
দুইয়ের সংযোগে লভি এ তত্ত্বমঙ্গল।।

śrī nāma nāmī eka tattva

maṅgala svarūpa viṣṇu para tattva hari |
aprākṛta svarūpete śrī-vraja-vihārī ||60||
tāṅra nāma rūpa guṇa līlā aprākṛta |
tāṅhāra svarūpa haite bhinna nahe tattva ||61||
nāma nāmī eka tattva aprākṛta dharma |
e jaḍa jagate tāra nāhi āche marma ||62||
ei śuddha jñāna lābha bhakti bale haya |
tarke bahu dūra ihā jāniha niścaya ||63||
nija śuddha sādhana āra sādhu guru bala |
duiyera saṁyoge labhi e tattva maṅgala ||64||

Lord's name, form, qualities and pastimes are completely transcendental and non-different from Him. Both the Holy Name, nāma, and the possessor of the Name, nāmi, are one. Both are on the platform of eternal existence, eternal knowledge, and eternal bliss. This is the Absolute nature of Kṛṣṇa and His name.

This transcendental understanding can only be attained through devotional service and never by mundane logic and argument.

To attain the perfectional stage of Krisna consciousness, one has to rigidly execute the principles of devotional service under the shelter of the spiritual master and saintly devotees.

এই তত্ত্বসিদ্ধি যত দিন নাহি হয়।
ততদিন প্রাকৃতবুদ্ধি কভু না ছাড়য়।।
ততদিন নাম করি, না পাই স্বরূপ।
নামাভাসমাত্র হয় ভজনবিরূপ।।
বহু যত্নে লভ ভাই স্বরূপের সিদ্ধি।

শুদ্ধনামোচ্চারে পাবে পরংপদ-বুদ্ধি।।
যত্নসহ নিরন্তর নামাভাসে হরি।
নামেতে স্বরূপসিদ্ধি দিবে কৃপা করি'।।

ei tattva siddhi yata dina nāhi haya |
tata dina prākṛta buddhi kabhu nā chāḍaya ||65||
tata dina nāma kari nā pāi svarūpa |
nāmābhāsa mātra haya bhajana virūpa ||66||
bahu yatne labha bhāi svarūpa siddhi |
śuddha nāmoccāre pābe paraṁ pada buddhi ||67||
yatna saha nirantara nāmābhāse hari |
nāmete svarūpa siddhi dibe kṛpā kari ||68||

Until one attains this perfectional stage, he can not transcend material consciousness nor realize his constitutional position in the spiritual world.

Instead he remains on the platform of nāmābhāsa, which is a intermediary stage between offensive and pure chanting.

But if he continues diligently, he can reach the ultimate perfectional stage of attaining Kṛṣṇa's lotus feet by chanting the name purely.

কৃষ্ণ সর্ব্বেশ্বর, শিবাদি তাঁহার অংশ

সর্ব্বেশ্বর কৃষ্ণ, তাহে জানিবে নিশ্চয়।
শিবাদি দেবতা তাঁ'র অংশরূপ হয়।।
সেই সেই দেবের নামাদি গুণরূপ।
কৃষ্ণশক্তিদত্ত সিদ্ধ জানহ স্বরূপ।।
এরূপ জানিলে শিববিষ্ণুতে অভেদে।
জন্মিবে স্বরূপবুদ্ধি, গায় সর্ব্ববেদে।।
ভেদবুদ্ধি অপরাধ যত্নেতে ত্যজিবে।
গুরুকৃপাবলে তবে শ্রীনাম ভজিবে।।

kṛṣṇa sarveśvara śivādi tāṅhāra aṁśa

sarveśvara kṛṣṇa tāhe jānibe niścaya |
śivādi devatā tāṅra aṁśa rūpa haya ||69||
sei sei devera nāmādi guṇa rūpa |
kṛṣṇa śakti datta siddha jānaha svarūpa ||70||
e rūpa jānile śiva viṣṇute abhede |
janmibe svarūpa buddhi gāya sarva vede ||71||
bheda buddhi aparādha yatnete tyajibe |
guru kṛpā bale tabe śrī nāma bhajibe ||72||

Lord Kṛṣṇa is the Supreme Absolute Truth, controller and master of all the demigods like Lord Śiva and Lord Brahma. These demigods are His parts and parcels. These demigods' names, forms and powers emanate from the transcendental potencies of Lord Kṛṣṇa.

When one is situated on the platform of knowledge, he realises that the Supreme Lord Viṣṇu and Lord Śiva are qualitatively one and the same. The demigods can never be on the same level as the Supreme Lord.

One should carefully avoid this offense and advance on the path of chanting the holy name by the mercy of the guru.

"গুরোরবজ্ঞা শ্রুতিশাস্ত্রনিন্দনং
তথার্থবাদো হরিনাম্নি কল্পনম্।
নাম্নো বলাদ্যস্য হি পাপবুদ্ধি-
র্ন বিদ্যতে তস্য যমৈর্হি শুদ্ধিঃ।।" ৯।।

guror avajñā śrutiśāstranindanam
tathārthavādo harināmni kalpanam |
nāmno balād yasya hi pāpabuddhir
na vidyate tasya yamair hi śuddhiḥ ||9||73||

This sloka is explained in the following verses.

গুরু-কর্ণধারের অনাদর

কৃপা করি' যেই জন হরি দেখাইল।
হরিনাম-পরিচয় করাইয়া দিল।।
সেই মোর কর্ণধার গুরু মহাশয়।
তাঁহারে অবজ্ঞা কৈলে নামাপরাধ হয়।।
'হীনজাতি, পাণ্ডিত্যরহিত, মন্ত্রহীন'।
নামের গুরুতে হেন বুদ্ধি অর্ব্বাচীন।।

guru karṇadhārera anādara

kṛpā kari yei jana hari dekhāila |
hari nāma paricaya karāiyā dila ||74||
sei mora karṇadhāra guru mahāśaya |
tāṅhāre avajñā kaile nāmāparādha haya ||75||
hīna jāti pāṇḍitya rahita mantra hīna |
nāmera gurute hena buddhi arvācīna ||76||

Disobeying the spiritual master:

By the mercy of the spiritual master, one attains the Supreme Lord Hari. By his mercy, a conditioned soul reestablishes his lost relationship with the Supreme Lord. The spiritual master mercifully introduces him to the process of chanting of the holy name.

Such a perfect spiritual master is like the helmsman for the conditioned soul, steering the boat of his life across the ocean of nescience. To disrespect and disobey him is a serious offense against the holy name.

Only a fool will judge such a spiritual master on material considerations such as birth in a lower family or lack of expertise in chanting of Vedic mantras etc.

শ্রুতিশাস্ত্রে অনাদর

যেই শ্রুতিশাস্ত্র নামের ব্রহ্মত্ব দেখায়।
অপার মাহাত্ম্য নামের জগতে জানায়।।
তা'রে অনাদর করি' কর্ম্মাদি প্রশংসে।
শ্রুতিনিন্দা বলি' তা'রে সর্ব্বশাস্ত্রে ভাষে।।

śruti śāstre anādara

yei śruti śāstra nāmera brahmatva dekhāya |
apāra māhātmya nāmera jagate jānāya ||77||
tāre anādara kari karmādi praśaṁse |
śruti nindā bali tāre sarva śāstre bhāṣe ||78||

Disrespecting the Vedic Literatures:

Vedic literatures such as the four Vedas and the Purāṇas unequivocally establish the transcendental nature of the holy name and propagate its wondrous glories in the world.

It is therefore a serious offense to blaspheme these Vedic literatures and glorify the process of fruitive activities as propounded in the karma-kanda section of the Vedas.

নামে কল্পনাবুদ্ধি

নাম নিত্যধন সদা চিন্ময় অগাধ।
তাহাতে কল্পনাবুদ্ধি গুরু অপরাধ।।

nāme kalpanā buddhi

nāma nitya dhana sadā cinmaya agādha |

tāhāte kalpanā buddhi guru aparādha ||79||

Considering the glories of the holy name imaginary:

The holy name of Kṛṣṇa is completely spiritual and an eternal priceless treasure for the living entiry. To consider the name and its transcendental qualities as imaginary is a serious nāmāparādha.

নামবলে পাপবুদ্ধি

নামবলে পাপবুদ্ধি হৃদয়ে যাহার।
সতত উদয় হয়, সেই ত' অসার।।

nāma bale pāpa buddhi

nāma bale pāpa buddhi hṛdaye yāhāra |
satata udaya haya sei ta asāra ||80||

Committing sin on the strength of the chanting:

The next nāmāparādha is to commit sin on the strength of the chanting of the holy name. This mentality renders all devotional performances ineffective and useless.

নামে অর্থবাদ

রোচনার্থা ফলশ্রুতি কর্ম্মমার্গে সত্য।
ভক্তিমার্গে নামফল সর্ব্বকালে নিত্য।।
অপ্রাকৃত নামের মাহাত্ম্য সীমাহীন।
তা'তে যা'র 'অর্থবাদ' সেই অর্ব্বাচীন।।

nāme artha vāda

rocanārthā phala śruti karma mārge satya |
bhakti mārge nāma phala sarva kāle nitya ||81||
aprākṛta nāmera māhātmya sīmā hīna |
tāte yāra artha vāda sei arvācīna ||82||

Interpreting the holy name:

Only fleeting pleasures are accrued as a result of performing fruitive activities recommended in the karma-kāṇḍa section of the Vedas. But by chanting the holy name within the realm of bhakti, one receives the benedictions which are eternal.

The transcendental glories of the holy name are unlimited. To give some mundane interpretation on the holy name, considering it's glories an exaggeration is an offense.

এই সব অপরাধ বর্জ্জনে নামের কৃপা

এই পঞ্চ অপরাধ বর্জ্জিবে যতনে।
তবে ত' নামের কৃপা লভিবে সাধনে।।

ei saba aparādha varjane nāmera kṛpā

ei pañca aparādha varjibe yatane |
tabe ta nāmera kṛpā labhibe sādhane ||83||

These five offenses should be avoided with great care. Only then can an aspiring devotee attract the mercy of the holy name.

"ধর্ম্মব্রতত্যাগহুতাদিসর্ব্বশুভক্রিয়াসাম্যমপি প্রমাদঃ।
অশ্রদ্দধানে বিমুখেঽপ্যশৃণ্বতি যশ্চোপদেশঃ
শিবনামাপরাধঃ।।" ১০

dharmavratatyāgahutādisarva
śubhakriyāsāmyam api pramādaḥ |
aśraddadhāne vimukhe'py aśṛṇvati
yaś copadeśaḥ śivanāmāparādhaḥ ||10|| 84||

This verse is explained in the following verses by the Lord.

সর্ব্ব শুভকর্ম্ম প্রাকৃত

বর্ণাশ্রমময়-ধর্ম্ম ধর্ম্মশাস্ত্রে যত।
দর্শপৌর্ণমাসী-আদি তমোময়-ব্রত।।
দণ্ডী মুণ্ডী সন্ন্যাসাদি ত্যাগের প্রকার।
নিত্য নৈমিত্তিক হোম-আদির ব্যাপার।।
অষ্টাঙ্গ-ষড়ঙ্গ-যোগ-আদি শুভ-কর্ম্ম।
সকলই প্রাকৃত-তত্ত্ব, এই সত্য মর্ম্ম।।
উপায়রূপেতে তা'রা উপেয় সাধয়।
না সাধিলে জড় বই কিছু আর নয়।।

sarva śubha karma prākṛta

varṇāśrama maya dharma dharma śāstre yata |
darśa paurṇamāsī ādi tamo maya vrata ||85||
daṇḍī muṇḍī sannyāsādi tyāgera prakāra |
nitya naimittika homa ādira vyāpāra ||86||
aṣṭāṅga ṣaḍ-aṅga yoga ādi śubha karma |
sakala-i prākṛta tattva ei satya marma ||87||
upāya rūpete tāra upeya sādhaya |
nā sādhile jaḍa bai kichu āra naya ||88||

All mundane pious activities are material:

Mundane pious activities are the duties recommended in the sections of the scriptures which enunciate varṇāśrama system and its religious practices. There are various systems of fasting, renunciation by taking sannyāsa, living as a mendicant, performing daily fire sacrifices and the different branches of yogic practices. These may be considered pious but are factually not spiritual.

These processes are meant to help a practitioner achieve a higher goal, but if the aspiration to attain the supreme objective Kṛṣṇa is missing, then these processes are nothing but mundane pious activities.

শ্রীনাম উপায়, উপেয়

নাম কিন্তু অপ্রাকৃত চিন্ময় ব্যাপার।
সাধনে উপায়তত্ত্ব, সাধ্যে উপেয়-সার।।
অতএব নামতত্ত্ব বিশুদ্ধ চিন্ময়।
জড়োপায় কর্ম্ম সহ সাম্য কভু নয়।।

śrī nāma upāya upeya

nāma kintu aprākṛta cinmaya vyāpāra |
sādhane upāya tattva sadhye upeya sāra ||89||
ata eva nāma tattva viśuddha cinmaya |
jaḍopāya karma saha sāmya kabhu naya ||90||

Holy name is the means and the goal at the same time:

Chanting the holy name of Krishna on the other hand, is a completely transcendental activity.

On the stage of practice or 'sadhana,' the holy name is the only means (upaya) to reach the supreme absolute goal, Kṛṣṇa. But when perfection in chanting is attained by chanting the holy name purely ('upeya'), then chanting itself becomes the end (sadhya). Therefore, the holy name and the chanting process are both transcendental, supremely spiritual and impossible to realize through any fruitive, mundane pursuits.

কর্ম্মজ্ঞান সহ নাম তুল্য নহে

কর্ম্মজ্ঞান সহ নামে সাম্যবুদ্ধি যথা।
নাম-অপরাধ গুরুতর ঘটে তথা।।

karma jñāna saha nāma tulya nahe

karma jñāna saha nāme sāmya buddhi yathā |
nāma aparādha gurutara ghaṭe tathā ||91||

To considering the chanting of the holy name on the same level as cultivation of material knowledge and performance of fruitive activities is a serious offense.

অবিশ্বাসী জনে নাম উপদেশ

নামে যা'র বিশ্বাস না জন্মিল ভাগ্যাভাবে।
তা'কে নাম উপদেশি' অপরাধ পাবে।।
এই দুই অপরাধ সদ্‌গুরুকৃপায়।
বহু যত্নে ছাড়ি' ভাই নামধন পায়।।

aviśvāsī jane nāma upadeśa

nāme yāra viśvāsa nā janmila bhāgyābhāve |
tāke nāma upadeśi aparādha pābe ||92||
ei dui aparādha sad-guru-kṛpāya |
bahu yatne chāḍi bhāi nāma dhana pāya ||93||

Instructing the faithless in chanting of the holy name:

Another nāmāparādha is to instruct persons who, due to

insufficient piety, have not been able to develop faith in the holy name.

Only by the mercy of a bona fide spiritual master can one rid himself of these two formidable offenses. At that time it will be possible to achieve perfection in chanting.

"শ্রুত্বাপি নামমাহাত্ম্যং যঃ প্রীতিরহিতোঽধম।
অহং-মমাদিপরমো নাম্নি সোঽপ্যপরাধকৃৎ।।" ১১।।

śrute'pi nāmamāhātmye yaḥ prītirahito'dhamaḥ |
ahaṁ mamādiparamo nāmni so'py aparādhakṛt ||11||94||

This verse is analyzed in the following verses.

নামের মাহাত্ম্য সব শুনি' শাস্ত্র হৈতে।
তবু তাহে রতি যার নৈল কোনমতে।।
অহংতা-মমতা-বুদ্ধি দেহেতে করিয়া।
লাভ-পূজা-প্রতিষ্ঠাতে রহিল মজিয়া।।
পাপে রত হঞা পাপ ছাড়িতে না পারে।
নামে যত্ন করি' চেষ্টা করিবারে নারে।।

nāmera māhātmya saba śuni śāstra haite |
tabu tāhe rati yāra naila kona mate ||95||
ahaṁtā mamatā buddhi dehete kariyā |
lābha pūjā pratiṣṭhāte rahila majiyā ||96||
pāpe rata hañā pāpa chāḍite nā pāre |
nāme yatna kari ceṣṭā karibāre nāre ||97||

Even after hearing the pristine glories of the holy name from revealed scriptures, a person may not develop attachment for the holy name. This is due to his polluted intelligence, engrossed in the bodily conception of I and mine, such a person's life is dedicated to the pursuits of profit, adoration, and distinction. Addicted to sinful activities, he cannot give them up and makes no attempt to chant the holy name even with a little sincerity.

সাধুসঙ্গে মতি নহে অসাধু বিষয়ে।
সুখ পায় বিবেক বৈরাগ্য ছাড়াইয়ে।।
এই ত' নামাপরাধ ঘটনা তাহার।
নামে রুচি নাহি পায় কৃষ্ণের সংসার।।
এই দশ অপরাধ নামাপরাধ হয়।
নামধর্ম্মে বাধা দেয় সুমঙ্গলক্ষয়।।

sādhu saṅge mati nahe asādhu viṣaye |
sukha pāya viveka vairāgya chāḍāiye ||98||
ei ta nāmāparādha ghaṭanā tāhāra |
nāme ruci nāhi pāya kṛṣṇera saṁsāra ||99||
ei daśa aparādha nāmāparādha haya |
nāma dharme bādhā deya sumaṅgala kṣaya ||100||

He has no attraction for saintly association, and prefers the company of the depraved. He finds pleasure in following the dictates of his uncontrolled senses, rather than in self-restraint. His lower nature goads him to commit nāmāparādha, and he never develops a taste for chanting the holy name. Thus, he is debarred from joining the blissful family of Kṛṣṇa.

These are the ten offenses against the holy name which bar one from taking full shelter of the holy name and achieving complete auspiciousness in life.

"সর্ব্বাপরাধকৃদপি মুচ্যতে হরিসংশ্রয়ঃ।
হরেরপ্যপরাধান্ যঃ কুর্য্যাদ্দ্বিপদপাংসনঃ।।
নামাশ্রয়ঃ কদাচিৎ স্যাত্তরত্যেষ স নামতঃ।
নাম্নো হি সর্ব্বসুহৃদো হ্যপরাধাৎ পতত্যধঃ।।

sarvāparādha-kṛd api mucyate hari-saṁśrayaḥ |
harer apy aparādhān yaḥ kuryād dvipāda pāṁsanaḥ |101||
nāmāśrayaḥ kadācit syāt taraty eṣa sa nāmataḥ |
nāmno hi sarva-suhṛdo hy aparādhāt pataty adhaḥ ||12||102||

This Sanskrit verse is explained by the following Bengali verses.

পাপ তাপ অপরাধ জীবের যত হয়।
শ্রীহরিসংশ্রয়ে সব সদ্য হয় ক্ষয়।।

কলির সংসার ছাড়িয়া কৃষ্ণের সংসার কর

কলির সংসার ছাড়ি' কৃষ্ণের সংসার।
অকৈতব করে যেই অপরাধ নাহি তা'র।।

pāpa tāpa aparādha jīvera yata haya |
śrī-hari-saṁśraye saba sadya haya kṣaya ||103||

kalira saṁsāra chāḍiyā kṛṣṇera saṁsāra kara

kalira saṁsāra chāḍi kṛṣṇera saṁsāra |
akaitave kare yei aparādha nāhi tāra ||104||

All sinful reactions, sufferings and offenses of the jīva are immediately destroyed as soon as he comes under the shelter of the Supreme Lord.

At this point, the jīva develops distaste for material existence, and because he is gradually becoming free from his offenses, he joins Kṛṣṇa's family of devotees without ulterior motive.

অকৈতবে করে যবে আত্মনিবেদন।
কৃষ্ণ তা'র পূর্ব্ব পাপ করেন খণ্ডন।।
প্রায়শ্চিত্ত করিবারে তা'র নাহি হয়।
দীক্ষামাত্র পাপক্ষয় সর্ব্বশাস্ত্রে কয়।।
নিষ্কপটে হর্ষাশ্রয় করে যেই জন।
সর্ব্ব অপরাধ তা'র বিনষ্ট তখন।।
আর পাপতাপে কভু রুচি নাহি হয়।
পুনঃ পাপ দূরে যায়, মায়া করে জয়।।

akaitave kare yabe ātma-nivedana |
kṛṣṇa tāra pūrva pāpa karena khaṇḍana ||105||
prāyaścitta karibāre tāra nāhi haya |
dīkṣā mātra pāpa kṣaya sarva śāstre kaya ||106||
niṣkapaṭe harṣāśraya kare yei jana |
sarva aparādha tāra vinaṣṭa takhana ||107||
āra pāpa tāpe kabhu ruci nāhi haya |
punaḥ pāpa dūre yāya māyā kare jaya ||108||

When jīva fully surrenders unto Kṛṣṇa, without any duplicity, Kṛṣṇa deliver him from all sinful reactions. He does not have to undergo any ritualistic atonement. According to the scriptural verdict, simply by receiving initiation from a bona fide spiritual master, he becomes freed from all sinful reactions.

From the moment of sincere surrender, he no longer delights in sinful, sensual pleasures. The desire to sin becomes further weakened, and he conquers over māyā (illusion).

সেবা অপরাধ

তবে তা'র কভু হয় সেবা-অপরাধ।
সেই অপরাধে হয় ভক্তিক্রিয়াবাধ।।
সাধুসঙ্গে করে কৃষ্ণনামের আশ্রয়।
নামাশ্রয়ে সেবা-অপরাধ নষ্ট হয়।।
নামকৃপা হৈলে জীব সর্ব্বশুদ্ধি পায়।
কৃষ্ণের নিকট গিয়া কর শুদ্ধসেবার আশ্রয়।।

sevā-aparādha

tabe tāra kabhu haya sevā aparādha |
sei aparādhe haya bhakti kriyā bādha ||109||
sādhu saṅge kare kṛṣṇa nāmera āśraya |
nāmāśraye sevā aparādha naṣṭa haya ||110||
nāma kṛpā haile jīva sarva śuddhi pāya |
kṛṣṇera nikaṭa giyā kare śuddha sevāra āśraya ||111||

Offenses while performing devotional service:

Thereafter, the jīva may accidentally commit some offenses in the execution of devotional service, known as sevaparadha. These offenses prevent the supremely purifying process of devotional service from taking full effect.

To counteract these offenses, one must take the shelter of the holy name in the association of saintly devotees. By such shelter, the offenses are mitigated.

The holy name purifies jiva from all sinful reactions and enables him to render pure devotional service unto Kṛṣṇa in His direct association.

সর্ব্বদা নামাপরাধ বর্জ্জনীয়

কিন্তু যদি নাম-অপরাধ তা'র হয়।
তবে পুনঃ অধঃপাত হইবে নিশ্চয়।।
সর্ব্বজীব-বন্ধু নাম, তাঁ'র অপরাধ।
কোনক্রমে ক্ষয় নহে প্রাপ্ত্যে হয় বাধ।।
নাম অপরাধ ত্যাগ বহু যত্নে করি'।
লভে জীব সর্ব্বসিদ্ধি প্রাপ্ত হয় হরি।।

sarvadā nāmāparādha varjanīya

kintu yadi nāma aparādha tāra haya |
tabe punaḥ adhaḥ pāta haibe niścaya ||112||
sarva jīva bandhu nāma tāṅra aparādha |
kona krame kṣaya nahe prāptye haya bādha ||113||
nāma aparādha tyāga bahu yatne kari |
labhe jīva sarva siddhi prāpta haya hari ||114||

Offenses to the holy name must always be avoided:

And if inadvertently one commits nāmāparādha, he certainly falls down from the spiritual platform.

The holy name is jīva's greatest well-wishing friend, so any offense against the holy name can almost never be exonerated. Hence, one should take extreme care to avoid offenses against the holy name, and in this way perfect one's existence by attaining the lotus feet of Hari.

"এবং নারদঃ শঙ্করেণ কৃপয়া মহ্যং মুনীনাং পরং
প্রোক্তং নাম সুখাবহং ভগবতো বর্জ্জ্যং সদা যত্নতঃ।।
যে জ্ঞাত্বাপি ন বর্জ্জয়ন্তি সহসা নামাপরাধান্দশ।
ক্রুদ্ধা মাতরমপ্যভোজনপরাঃ খিদ্যন্তি তে বালবৎ।।" ১৩।।

evam nāradaḥ saṇkarena krpayā maḥyam munināṁ paraṁ
proktam nāma sukhāvaham bhagavato varjyam sada yatnataḥ
ye jñātvapi na varjayanti sahasā nāmāparādhāndaśa
kruddhā mātaramapyabhojana parāḥ khidyanti te balavat
||13||115||

This sloka is explained by the following verses.

আমি পূর্ব্বে শিবলোকে শঙ্করসন্নিধানে।
নাম-অপরাধ-কথা জিজ্ঞাসিলাম মুনে।।
বহুমুনিগণ মধ্যে শম্ভু কৃপা করি।
আমায় উপদেশ করে কৈলাস উপরি।।
ভগবানের নাম সর্ব্বজীবসুখাবহ।
তা'তে অপরাধ সর্ব্ব-অমঙ্গল-বহ।।
মঙ্গল লভিতে যা'র ইচ্ছা আছে মনে।
সদা নাম-অপরাধ বর্জ্জিবে যতনে।।

āmi pūrve śiva loke śaṅkara-sannidhāne |
nāma aparādha kathā jijñāsilāma mune ||116||
bahu muni gaṇa madhye śambhu kṛpā kari |
āmāya upadeśa kare kailāsa upari ||117||
bhagavānera nāma sarva jīva sukhāvaha |
tāte aparādha sarva amaṅgala vaha ||118||
maṅgala labhite yāra icchā āche mane |
sadā nāma aparādha varjibe yatane ||119||

Long ago I placed this same question on nāmāparādha before Lord Siva in his abode, Sivaloka. There, on Mount Kailasa in the presence of many great sages, he mercifully instructed me.

The Lord's holy name is the source of transcendental bliss for the jīva. Offense against the holy name brings about great inauspiciousness in life. One who desires the highest benefit for himself will carefully avoid nāmāparādha.

সাধুগুরুসন্নিধানে বহু দৈন্য ধরি'।
দশ অপরাধ-তত্ত্ব লবে শিক্ষা করি'।।
অপরাধগুলি যত্নে জানিয়া ত্যজিবে।
সত্বরে শ্রীহরিনামে প্রেম উপজিবে।।
নাম পেয়ে অপরাধ বর্জ্জন না করে।
সহসা তাহারে দশ অপরাধ ধরে।।

sādhu guru sannidhāne bahu dainya dhari |
daśa aparādha tattva labe śikṣā kari ||120||
aparādha guli yatne jāniyā tyajibe |
satvare śrī-hari-nāme prema upajibe ||121||
nāma peye aparādha varjana nā kare |
sahasā tāhāre daśa aparādha dhare ||122||

He humbly approaches his guru and other advanced Vaiṣṇavas to learn from them how to avoid the ten nāmāparādhas. Then he takes extreme care to avoid ten offenses and very soon he develops attachment for the holy name and comes to the perfectional stage.

On the other hand, if he is careless after being instructed about the chanting of the holy name, he might come under the ominous shadow of the ten offenses.

অপরাধ বর্জ্জন না করিয়া নাম করা মূঢ়তা

অপরাধ বুঝিয়া যে বর্জ্জনে উদাসীন।
তা'র দুঃখ নিরন্তর, সেই অর্ব্বাচীন।।
মায়ে ক্রোধ করি' বালক না করে ভোজন।

সুপথ্য অভাবে সদা ক্লেশের ভাজন।।
সেইরূপ অপরাধ বর্জ্জন না করি'।
নাম করে মূঢ় নিজ শিব পরিহরি'।।

aparādha varjana nā kariyā nāma karā mūḍhatā

aparādha bujhiyā ye varjane udāsīna |
tāra duḥkha nirantara sei arvācīna ||123||
māye krodha kari bālaka nā kare bhojana |
supathya abhāve sadā kleśera bhājana ||124||
sei rūpa aparādha varjana nā kari |
nāma kare mūḍha nija śiva parihari ||125||

One who is complacent about ten offenses in spite of having a clear understanding of them, such a fool drowns in the whirlpool of distress. A child who refuses to eat just because he is angry with his mother, will naturally be malnourished and susceptible to diseases. In the same way, a fool may chant while not caring for the offenses but he is just neglecting his spiritual wellbeing.

"অপরাধবিমুক্তো হি নাম্নি জপ্তং সদাচার।
নাম্নৈব তব দেবর্ষে সর্ব্বাং সেৎস্যতি নান্যথা।।

aparādha-vimukto hi nāmni japtaṁ sadācara |
nāmnaiva tava devarṣe sarvāṁ setsyati nānyathā ||14||126||

This Sanskrit verse is explained in the following verses by the author.

সনৎকুমার বলে, 'ওহে দেবর্ষিপ্রবর।
নিরপরাধে নাম জপ সদাই আচর।।
নাম বিনা অন্য পন্থা নাহি প্রয়োজন।
নামেতে সকল সিদ্ধি পাবে তপোধন।।

sanat kumāra bale ohe devarṣi pravara |
niraparādha nāma japa sadā ācara ||127||
nāma vinā anya panthā nāhi prayojana |
nāmete sakala siddhi pābe tapo-dhana ||128||

Sanatkumāra said, 'O Devarsi Nārada: The proper way to chant the holy name is by avoiding the ten offenses. There is no need for any other process of spiritual realization, for the holy name alone can bring one to the perfectional stage.

শ্রীনারদ উবাচ
"সনৎকুমার প্রিয় সাহসানাং
বিবেক-বৈরাগ্যবিবর্জ্জিতানাম্।
দেহপ্রিয়ার্থাত্ম্যপরায়ণানা-
মুক্তাপরাধাঃ প্রভবন্তি নো কথম্।।

śrī-nārada uvāca—
sanat-kumāra priya sāhasānāṁ
viveka-vairāgya-vivarjitānām |
deha-priyārthātmya-parāyaṇānām
uktāparādhāḥ prabhavanti no katham ||15||129||

Śrī Nārada's reply in this verse is explained in the following verses.

ওহে সনৎকুমার! তুমি সিদ্ধ হরিদাস।
অনায়াসে করিলে নামরহস্যপ্রকাশ।।

সাধকের নামাপরাধ বর্জ্জনোপায়

সাধক আমরা আমাদের বড় ভয়।
অপরাধ-ত্যাগে যত্ন কিরূপেতে হয়।।
বিষয় মোদের বন্ধু তাহার সাহসে।
করিবে সকল কর্ম্ম বদ্ধ মায়াপাশে।।
বিবেকবৈরাগ্যশূন্য দেহ প্রিয়জন।
অর্থস্বরূপে মোরা সদা পরায়ণ।।
কিরূপে সাধক-মনে অপরাধ দশ।
নাহি উপজিবে তাহা করহ প্রকাশ।।

ohe sanatkumāra tumi siddha haridāsa |
anāyāse karile nāma rahasya prakāśa ||130||

sādhakera nāmāparādha varjanopāya

sādhaka āmarā āmādera baḍa bhaya |
aparādha tyāge yatna ki rūpete haya ||131||
viṣaya modera bandhu tāhāra sāhase |
karibe sakala karma baddha māyā pāśe ||132||
viveka vairāgya śūnya deha priya jana |
artha svarūpe morā sadā parāyaṇa ||133||
ki rūpe sādhaka mane aparādha daśa |
nāhi upajibe tāha karaha prakāśa ||134||

O Sanatkumāra! You are a topmost devotee of the Supreme Lord, so you could elucidate the esoteric truth about the holy name. We are all simply practitioners and we are afraid that we may not commit offenses.

We are attached to sense gratification and are caught up in the illusory network of maya. Bereft of intelligence and discrimination, we are attached to this temporary body and its byproducts, our kinsmen.

For us money is sweeter than honey. Pray tell us how we can root out the slightest possibility of committing the ten offenses.

শ্রীসনৎকুমার উবাচ
জাতে নামাপরাধে তু প্রমাদে বৈ কথঞ্চন।
সদা সঙ্কীর্ত্তয়েন্নাম তদেকশরণো ভবেৎ।।
নামাপরাধযুক্তানি নামান্যেব হরন্ত্যঘম্।
অবিশ্রান্তপ্রযুক্তানি তান্যেবার্থকরাণি হি।।

śrī-sanatkumāra uvāca—
jāte nāmāparādhe'pi pramādena kathañcana |
sadā saṅkīrtayan nāma tad-eka-śaraṇo bhavet ||135||
nāmāparādha-yuktānāṁ nāmāny eva haranty agham |
aviśrānta-prayuktāni tāny evārtha-karāṇi ca ||16||136||

Śrī Sanatkumāra's reply is explain in the following verses.

নামেতে শরণাপত্তি যেই ক্ষণে হয়।
তখনই নামাপরাধের সদ্য হয় ক্ষয়।।
তথাপি প্রমাদে যদি উঠে অপরাধ।
তাহাতেও ভক্তিতে হইয়া পড়ে বাধ।।
অপরাধ প্রমাদেতে হইবে যখন।
নামসংকীর্ত্তন তবে করিবে অনুক্ষণ।।
নামেতে শরণাগতি সুদৃঢ় করিবে।
অনুক্ষণ নামবলে অপরাধ যাবে।।

nāmete śaraṇāpatti yei kṣaṇe haya |
takhana-i nāmāparādhera sadya haya kṣaya ||137||
tathāpi pramāde yadi uṭhe aparādha |
tāhāte-o bhaktite haiyā paḍe bādha ||138||

aparādha pramādete haibe yakhana |
nāma-saṅkīrtana tabe karibe anukṣaṇa ||139||
nāmete śaraṇāgati sudṛḍha karibe |
anukṣaṇa nāma bale aparādha yābe ||140||

As soon as a person humbly surrenders to the holy name (the holy name and Kṛṣṇa being non-different), all his offenses are immediately nullified. Yet, if due to negligence, he happens to commit an offense once again, it jeopardise his progress in bhakti.

The only way to counteract this offense is to chant continuously. By such continuous and intensified chanting, one should augment his surrender to the holy name. Then he will be relieved of the offense to the holy name.

নামই উপায়

নামেই নামাপরাধ হইবেক ক্ষয়।
অপরাধ নাশিতে আর কারও শক্তি নয়।।
এ বিষয়ে মূলতত্ত্ব বলি হে তোমায়।
বুঝহ নারদ ! তুমি বেদে যাহা গায়।।

nāma-i upāya

nāme-i nāmāparādha haibeka kṣaya |
aparādha nāśite āra kāra-o śakti naya ||141||
e viṣaye mūla-tattva bali he tomāya |
bujhaha nārada tumi vede yāhā gāya ||142||

Chanting is the only means:

Chanting is the only way to mitigate the offenses to the holy name. Other than the holy name, no one else is capable of granting relief from these offenses. O Sage Nārada, let me explain you the essential truth about this subject which is elaborated in the Vedas.

নামৈকং যস্য বাচি স্মরণপথগতং শ্রোত্রমূলং গতং বা
শুদ্ধং বাশুদ্ধবর্ণং ব্যবহিতরহিতং তারয়ত্যেব সত্যম্।
তচ্চেদ্দেহ-দ্রবিণ-জনতা-লোভ-পাষণ্ড-মধ্যে
নিক্ষিপ্তং স্যান্নফলজনকং শীঘ্রমেবাত্র বিপ্র।। ১৭।।

nāmaikaṁ yasya vāci smaraṇa pathagataṁ śrotramūlaṁ gataṁ vā
śuddhaṁ vāśuddhavarṇaṁ vyavahitarahitaṁ tārayaty eva satyam |
tac ced dehadraviṇajanatālobhapāṣaṇḍamadhye
nikṣiptaṁ syān na phalajanakaṁ śīghram evātra vipra
||17||143||

The verse is explained in the following verses.

যা'র মুখে উচ্চারিত এক কৃষ্ণনাম ।
যাহার স্মরণপথে এক নাম গুণধাম।।
যা'র শ্রোত্রমূলে তাহা প্রবেশ করিবে।
ব্যবহিত-রহিত হৈলে তখনই তারিবে।।
'ব্যবহিত' এই শব্দে দুই অর্থ হয়।
অক্ষরের ব্যবধানে নাম আচ্ছাদয়।।
অবিদ্যার আচ্ছাদনে প্রাকৃত প্রকাশ।
নাম নামী একভাবে অবিদ্যা-বিনাশ।।
ব্যবহিত-রহিত হৈলে শুদ্ধনামোদয়।
বর্ণশুদ্ধাশুদ্ধিক্রমে দোষ নাহি হয়।।
অপ্রাকৃত নামে কৃষ্ণ সর্ব্বশক্তি দিল।
কালাকাল শৌচাশৌচ নামে না রহিল।।
সর্ব্বকাল সর্ব্বাবস্থায় শুদ্ধ নাম কর।
সর্ব্ব শুভোদয় হ'বে সর্ব্বাশুভ-হর।।

yāra mukhe uccārita eka kṛṣṇa nāma |
yāhāra smaraṇa pathe eka nāma guṇa dhāma ||144||
yāra śrotra mūle tāhā praveśa karibe |
vyavahita rahita haile takhana-i tāribe ||145||
vyavahita ei śabde dui artha haya |
akṣarera vyavadhāne nāma ācchādaya ||146||
avidyāra ācchādane prākṛta prakāśa |
nāma nāmī eka bhāve avidyā vināśa ||147||
vyavahita rahita haile śuddha nāmodaya |
varṇa-śuddhāśuddhi-krame doṣa nāhi haya ||148||
aprākṛta nāme kṛṣṇa sarva śakti dila |
kālākāla śaucāśauca nāme nā rahila ||149||
sarva kāla sarvāvasthāya śuddha nāma kara |
sarva śubhodaya habe sarvāśubha hara ||150||

If the holy name is chanted, remembered or heard even once without offenses or without being separated, then in a moment the holy name can liberate anyone.

The word vyavahita (separated, distance) has two meanings in this context. The holy name is obscured when the syllables are far apart or if it is chanted partially; secondly, when chanted in ignorance, one sees only the external, material form of the holy name. But when the holy name is chanted in full awareness of Its transcendental nature (i.e. the holy name, and the possessor of the holy name, the Supreme Lord are one and the same), then nescience is destroyed.

When these two discrepancies termed vyavahita are removed, pure name manifests.

There is no fault if diction, voice inflection and pronunciation are not perfect. In these transcendental names Kṛṣṇa has invested all His transcendental energies, and there are no hard and fast rules for chanting these names. There is no consideration of time, place, circumstance or clean or unclean state for chanting these names.

Simply chant the pure name at all times and under all circumstances. This is the most auspicious activity and it will drive away all inauspiciousness.

অসৎসঙ্গ ত্যাগপূর্ব্বক নাম-গ্রহণ

এমত অপূর্ব্ব-নাম সঙ্গযুক্ত যথা।
শীঘ্র শুভফলদাতা না হয় সর্ব্বথা।।
দেহ, ধন, জন, লোভ, পাষণ্ডসঙ্গক্রমে।
ব্যবহিত জন্মে, জীব পড়ে মহাভ্রমে।।
অতএব সকলের অগ্রে সঙ্গ ত্যজি'।
অনন্যশরণ লঞা নামমাত্র ভজি।।
নামকৃপাবলে হ'বে প্রমাদরহিত।
অপরাধ দূরে যা'বে, হইবেক হিত।।
অপরাধমুক্ত হঞা লয় কৃষ্ণনাম।
প্রেম আসি' নামসহ করিবে বিশ্রাম।।
অপরাধীর নামলক্ষণ কৈতব নিশ্চয়।
সে সঙ্গ যতনে ছাড়ি' কর নামাশ্রয়।।

asat saṅga tyāga pūrvaka nāma grahaṇa

emata apūrva nāma saṅga yukta yathā |
śīghra śubha phala dātā nā haya sarvathā ||151||
deha dhana jana lobha pāṣaṇḍa saṅga krame |
vyavahita janme jīva paḍe mahā bhrame ||152||
ata eva sakalera agre saṅga tyaji |
ananya śaraṇa lañā nāma mātra bhaji ||153||
nāma kṛpā bale habe pramāda rahita |
aparādha dūre yābe haibeka hita ||154||
aparādha mukta hañā laya kṛṣṇa nāma |
prema āsi nāma saha karibe viśrāma ||155||

aparādhīra nāma lakṣaṇa kaitava niścaya |
se saṅga yatane chāḍi kara nāmāśraya ||156||

When the sublime name is chanted in the company of devotees, only then does it give good results quickly but not otherwise. Due to close contact with atheists and materialists, the jīva becomes trapped in the illusory conceptions of body, wealth, relatives etc. and gives rise to improper or offensive chanting.

Therefore, his first step towards advancing in Kṛṣṇa consciousness should be to disassociate from non-devotees. Taking complete shelter of the holy name, he should simply chant. By the mercy of the holy name he becomes delivered from nescience; his offenses disappear, and he relishes the transcendental bliss of pure love.

An offensive chanter is invariably deceitful and capricious. His company should be carefully avoided.

ইদং রহস্যং পরমং পুরা নারদ শঙ্করাৎ।
শ্রুতং সর্ব্বাশুভহরমপরাধনিবারকম্।।
বিদুর্বিপ্রাভিধানং যে হ্যপরাধপরা নরাঃ।
তেষামপি ভবেন্মুক্তিঃ পঠনাদেব নারদ।।

idaṁ rahasyaṁ paramaṁ purā nārada śaṅkarāt |
śrutaṁ sarvāśubha-haram aparādha-nivārakam ||157||
vidur viprābhidhānaṁ ye hy aparādha-parā narāḥ |
teṣām api bhaven muktiḥ paṭhanād eva nārada ||18||158||

Following verses explain the meaning of this verse.

সনৎকুমার বলে,—"ওহে দেবর্ষিপ্রবর।
পূর্ব্বে শ্রীশঙ্কর মোরে হঞা দয়াপর।।
শ্রীনামরহস্য সর্ব্ব-অশুভ নাশন।
অপরাধ-নিবারক কৈল বিজ্ঞাপন।।
অপরাধপর জন বিষ্ণুনাম জানি'।
পাঠ করিলেই মুক্তি লভে ইহা মানি"।।

sanat-kumāra bale—ohe devarṣi pravara |
pūrve śrī-śaṅkara more hañā dayā para ||159||
śrī-nāma-rahasya sarva aśubha nāśana |
aparādha nivāraka kaila vijñāpana ||160||
aparādha para jana viṣṇu nāma jāni |
pāṭha karile-i mukti labhe ihā māni ||161||

Sanatkumāra said, O best of the sages Nārada, Lord Siva, showing great compassion, revealed the mysteries of the holy name to me. This transcendental knowledge at once dissipates all misgivings and mitigates all offenses.

Even those who are offensive can achieve liberation simply by chanting these transcendental names of the Lord.

নামরহস্যপটল প্রচার

ওহে স্বরূপ! রামরায়! এ নামরহস্য-
পটল যতনে প্রচার করিবে অবশ্য।।
কলিতে জীবের নাহি অন্য প্রতিকার।
নামরহস্যেতে পার হইবে সংসার।।
পূর্ব্বে মুঞি 'শিক্ষাষ্টকে'' যে তত্ত্ব কহিল।
এবে ব্যাসবাক্যে তাহা পুনঃ দেখাইল।।
যতনে রহস্যপটল প্রচারিবে সবে।
সর্ব্বক্ষণ আলোচিয়া নাম লবে তবে।।

nāma rahasya paṭala pracāra

ohe svarūpa rāma rāya e nāma rahasya
paṭala yatane pracāra karibe avaśya ||162||
kalite jīvera nāhi anya pratikāra |
nāma rahasyete pāra haibe saṁsāra ||163||
pūrve muñi śikṣāṣṭake ye tattva kahila |
ebe vyāsa-vākye tāhā punaḥ dekhāila ||164||
yatane rahasya paṭala pracāribe sabe |
sarva kṣaṇa ālociyā nāma labe tabe ||165||

Svarūpa Dāmodara! Rāmānanda Raya! It is imperative that you propagate the esoteric truth about the holy name with great care. The conditioned souls in Kali-yuga have no means of redemption other than to chant the holy name, realizing fully its superexcellent glories.

This transcendental knowledge, as revealed by Vyasadeva in these verses, was explained by me earlier in the form of the Siksastaka. Please broadcast this transcendental science far and wide, always discuss the wondrous glories of the holy name and chant incessantly.

নামাচার্য্য ঠাকুর হরিদাসের আনুগত্যে শ্রীনামভজন

পৃথিবীর শিরোমণি ছিল হরিদাস।
এই নামরহস্য সব করিল প্রকাশ।।
প্রচারিল আচরিল এই নামধর্ম্ম।
নামের আচার্য্য হরিদাস, জান মর্ম্ম।।
হরিদাসের অনুগত হইয়া শ্রীনাম।
ভজিবে যে জন সেই নিত্যসিদ্ধকাম।।

nāmācārya ṭhākura haridāsera ānugatye śrī nāma bhajana

pṛthivīra śiromaṇi chila haridāsa |
ei nāma rahasya saba karila prakāśa ||166||

pracārila ācarila ei nāma dharma |
nāmera ācārya haridāsa jāna marma ||167||
haridāsera anugata haiyā śrī nāma |
bhajibe ye jana sei nitya siddha kāma ||168||

Chant under the tutelage of Haridāsa Ṭhākura:

When it comes to chanting, the topmost devotee is Śrīla Haridāsa Ṭhākura, and it was he who propagated the transcendental science of the holy name. He practiced what he preached and hence he is the ācārya or the ordained minister of the holy name. Whoever chants the Lord's name following in his footsteps, will soon achieve the perfectional stage of pure love.

www.ingramcontent.com/pod-product-compliance
Lightning Source LLC
Chambersburg PA
CBHW070639030426
42337CB00020B/4083
* 9 7 8 9 3 8 2 9 4 7 1 6 5 *